11 10 09 08 07   5 4 3 2 1

Other fine Betterway Books are available from your local bookstore or at www.fwbookstore.com.

Distributed in Canada by Fraser Direct, 100 Armstrong Avenue, Georgetown, ON, Canada L7G 5S4, Tel: (905) 877-4411. Distributed in the U.K. and Europe by David & Charles, Brunel House, Newton Abbot, Devon, TQ12 4PU, England, Tel: (+44) 1626 323200, Fax: (+44) 1626 323319, E-mail: postmaster@davidandcharles.co.uk. Distributed in Australia by Capricorn Link, P.O. Box 704, Windsor, NSW 2756 Australia, Tel: (02) 4577-3555.

Library of Congress Cataloging-in-Publication Data
McCarthy, John P., 1947-
  Coaching youth football : the guide for coaches, parents and athletes / by John P. McCarthy, Jr. -- 3rd ed.
      p. cm.
  Rev. ed. of: The parent's guide to coaching football. 2nd ed.
  Includes index.
  ISBN 978-1-55870-792-4 (pbk. : alk. paper)
  1. Football for children--Coaching. I. McCarthy, John P., 1947- Parent's guide to coaching football. II. Title.

  GV959.55.C45M33 2007
  796.33207'7--dc22
                        2007005645

Edited by Michelle Ehrhard
Designed by Grace Ring
Illustrations by John Rizzo
Cover design by Sean Braemer and Claudean Wheeler
Cover photography by Christine Polomsky
Page layout by Eric West
Page Production coordinated by Mark Griffin

fW
F+W PUBLICATIONS, INC.

D0053122

REVISED & UPDATED

COACHING YOUTH FOOTBALL

THIRD EDITION

REVISED & UPDATE

COACHING YOUTH
FOOTBALL

THIRD EDITION

The Guide for Coaches, Parents and Athletes

John P. McCarthy, Jr.

FOREWORD BY MARVIN LEWIS,
HEAD COACH OF THE
CINCINNATI BENGALS

BETTERWAY BOOKS
Cincinnati, Ohio

DEDICATION

To Bill Cochrane.
Thanks, Coach.

ACKNOWLEDGMENTS

Special thanks to my photo models, Connor McCarthy and Billy Turk.

ABOUT THE AUTHOR

Jack McCarthy, like many Americans, is a sports enthusiast and has played and coached numerous sports all of his life. As a parent, and now grandparent, he knows that athletic competition builds self-confidence in young people. It also prepares them to handle life's challenges and teaches them how to succeed. The Betterway Coaching Kids series was developed by Jack to help parents and coaches ensure that their child's experience in sports is a positive one.

Jack is an attorney and works for the New Jersey Courts. He lives with his wife and family, which includes three children and four grandchildren, in Hillsborough, New Jersey. His other books in the series include titles on baseball, soccer, and basketball. He has also written *Baseball's All-Time Dream Team*.

TABLE OF CONTENTS

FOREWORD

By Marvin Lewis, Head Coach
of the Cincinnati Bengals

Football remains the number one "team sport" in our society today. It teaches young people accountability, responsibility, and dependability within the scope of every successful play. These are three personal traits that, once instilled in young people, give them an opportunity to be successful in the much bigger game of life.

Coaching Youth Football provides coaches and parents with a strong and sound game plan of fundamentals of the game. Teaching a strong foundation of fundamentals with the above personal traits enables our young people to have a sense of accomplishment for all endeavors in their future life on or off the athletic field.

I thank you for taking the time and responsibility to coach this great game. I remind you of the influence you will have on these young people; keep every day positive and win them over one play at a time.

INTRODUCTION

"I want to play football, Dad." My ten-year-old son had been thinking about it for a year or so and decided to go for it. I knew that he was beginning to sense the glory of the game, the popularity, the cheerleaders. I hadn't urged him to play football, as I did with other sports. One reason was that football starts in August, when I usually planned our vacation. Also, it's a much greater commitment than other sports, with practice or a game five days a week. I figured he would eventually try out in high school, but admittedly I had some trepidation about him playing before then, particularly while he was in his growth period, from ten to thirteen. Let's face it—it's a rough game. I played and was injured once. I have some old friends who are still hobbling around. I guess parents naturally get a bit anxious about their child being exposed to such rugged competition even though we did so ourselves.

Anyway, Joey chose to play, and my wife and I chose to support his decision. He signed up for a local Pop Warner team called the Dukes. Most of the other kids had already played for a few years, but Joe made the team and eventually won a starting position at fullback. I was happy to see that Pop Warner rules separate the kids so they play against other kids in the same age and weight class. Joe's weight qualified him for the Junior Midgets, which then was the 90 to 115-pound class. Interestingly, as I write this third edition of my football coaching book, I am helping my grandson as he begins his football experience, also with the 90 to 115-pound-class, now called the Pee Wees.

I noticed, as I watched Joey at practice and thought about the game more carefully, that there are dimensions to football that are very different from the other major sports. I looked around and found virtually no books geared both to beginners and to parents, as well as coaches. That's one problem I hope to resolve with this book.

The area in which kids seem to struggle most in football is in that all-important area of desire and confidence. More than skills, this game requires something from within. As I watched, it occurred to me that parents could be most helpful by trying to get their child properly motivated to play the game. I am repulsed by the way some coaches seem to preach violence to the kids, screaming, "Kill him! Go out there and hurt someone!" I also see far too much humiliation and insulting language coming from coaches. I know they are usually just trying to psych a kid up, but I can't see how such guidance is good for young boys. I understand that it's a tough game, but parents and coaches need to ensure that their players get a correct perspective. That's the second reason I wrote this book.

I have learned throughout my life—in sports, in my professional career, and in my family affairs—that at times things can get pretty rough. But just hanging in there, knowing how to hold on, is sometimes all it takes to make it. I have also learned that tough problems require concentrated effort and reaching down to give it all I've got. Most importantly, I've learned that I have something extra within me, intangible but always there, ready to help out. All sports teach these life lessons, yet it is football that seems to teach them best of all.

Football is not about violence, and it's not about a license to bully; it's about rising to a challenge and overcoming it. It's about finding that special, extra reserve we all have within us. This is the message of football, and it is the third and main reason for this book. If this book does nothing else, make sure that your players or child get that message. Help your son find the good in this game, and also help him to avoid the negatives.

This book is written in the masculine. It is merely a recognition of the obvious fact that extremely few girls play football, at any level. If you have a daughter in the game, I apologize. I don't mean to exclude—in fact, I discuss girls in football in chapter eight; however, it seemed senseless to write this book gender neutral since it is so very rare that girls play this sport.

Writing books about youth sports has been a most interesting and rewarding experience for me. Writing this book has given me a new perspective on football, and I hope that by sharing it, you will be able to help your child, as I have learned to help mine. Go for it!

—Jack McCarthy

DESIRE

This is the most important chapter in the book. Don't skip it just because the word "desire" seems obvious or abstract. Desire is the most important aspect of football for both the player and the parent. Without it, your child will probably sit on the bench or play poorly. With it, he will surely find the game an exciting experience.

A player will hear his coaches say countless times, "Football is 90 percent desire." I have to admit, when I played football that famous phrase sounded nice, but it initially rang hollow to me. I believed that the game was mainly about strength, but I was dead wrong! Desire is the essence of football. It may not be 90 percent, but it's at least two-thirds of the game. The rest is evenly divided between physicality (strength and quickness), and knowing and executing your plays (and don't forget proper form!).

If you can find a way to light the fire of desire in your players, you will have helped them in the most meaningful way possible. Watch a game with young players, and you'll see that some of the kids really stand out. They make aggressive tackles or crunching blocks. The better running backs really pop the line, moving low and hard, running with abandon. Other kids are just hanging in there, holding their own, giving enough effort to make a decent go of it. Still others seem to be standing around, trying to avoid contact. They are usually not on the field for very long.

The main difference between all three groups is desire. Of course, upper-body strength and speed are very helpful. But the weight restrictions in most youth leagues limit the physical differences. At the high-school level, the weight restrictions in place for grade-schoolers are removed, so sheer size then becomes quite valuable. But at all levels, the desire to get in the action and give a good jolt, separates the players from the substitutes. *Desire can easily equalize size and strength.* I've seen it happen countless times. If you can instill or increase this attitude in young men, they will improve their play far more than by weight training, conditioning, or learning basic skills.

WHAT IS FOOTBALL DESIRE?

Desire in football is the determination to overcome an opponent, whether by delivering a solid block, by thwarting an attempted block and going on to make the tackle, or by refusing to be tackled easily. Desire is not anger, is not personal, and does not involve or require intent to hurt someone. The opponent is merely an obstacle to overcome. (See figure 1-1.)

Desire is a state of mind, an abandonment of self, a form of courage, the joy of mixing it up, a sense of personal toughness. It is doing your very best, calling up whatever reserve power is available and never quitting. It is playing both for yourself and for the team. It is the exercise of a determined will flowing from a competitive spirit driven to achieve a goal.

The good news is that desire is available to all kids, not just a gifted few. Size and speed are a given for kids; they have what they got. But desire can be learned, and it can be coached. How good of a football coach you are depends on your success at coaching football desire. Sure, some kids will show up already fully motivated, tough kids who like to give a good jolt; it comes naturally to them. However, in many—perhaps most—this football desire is not as natural. Some kids are not aggressive by nature. It's not easy for an easygoing kid to really pop another kid, especially a schoolmate. In still others, desire is buried under a lack of self-confidence or maybe a lack of interest, and it

1-1. **DESIRE**

The essence of football is the desire to overcome one's individual opponent.

needs to be dug out and fired up. I know it can be. With desire comes success on the field, and this breeds self-confidence. The unfolding of confidence in a child is truly something to behold.

Football is quite different from other sports. As my other books for parents and coaches point out, hitting a baseball, dribbling a soccer ball, or shooting a basketball all require highly refined skills. Sports such as these require constant practice, repetition, and great concentration. While football certainly involves all of these, and I will discuss specific football skills in great detail later on, football is primarily a game of strength and rugged, one-on-one physical contact. The key to football lies more in the desire to overcome the individual opponent than in the development of individual skills. Great football teams have a great running game, and it's usually because their offensive lines are beating their opponents one-on-one.

Let me share with you a personal story. I didn't play football until high school; back in the late 1950s, there wasn't a Pop Warner team in my area. I started off as an offensive end, but I had trouble holding on to passes. While I was big and strong, I was a fairly gentle person, and so I was not consistently blocking well. My form was good, my strength was good, but I had no *gusto*. During practices, we ran plays against dummies (defensive players carrying big pads that we blocked into). One day, the assistant coach called a huddle and looked at me and said, "Well, Mac, you can't catch, and you don't pop the defense, so maybe you ought to just go and get me a drink of water." Well, it got my attention! I remember looking him in the eye, and I was quite upset. Whatever he saw, he let me stay in the huddle. On the next play, I went after a cornerback and hit into him with all I had. I knocked him 6 feet and he went right down on his back ... and that was with a big dummy pad to protect him! The coach saw it and called the same play in the next huddle. Same result: I knocked the kid on his butt again. After practice, Coach called me over and said, "You are now an offensive tackle, and if you keep hitting like that, you'll play with the first team."

Frankly, I was amazed that I could deliver such a jolt to a player. I realized that the ability was there for me any time I wanted to bring it to bear. I did not have to get angry. I just had to give each play my best effort.

EIGHT APPROACHES TO DEVELOPING DESIRE

The good news is that parents and coaches can help bring forth football desire by communicating and reinforcing certain concepts with their players. The unfortunate approach used by far too many coaches is to scream at or insult players to get them fired up. Sometimes it works, of course, but at what price? Football practices and games with these coaches are an emotional circus with too many people screaming their heads off. I don't believe this works for the kids who are most in need of getting fired up. Moreover, humiliating a kid often backfires and drives him away from the confidence he needs to give his best.

If a player is already highly motivated, then there may be little need to increase his desire. He has won more than half the battle, and the joy of the game will be his. However, particularly at the very young ages, most kids are at least a bit hesitant about the game, and they can benefit greatly from some communication. Talk it over. Here are some approaches to consider.

1. Talk about it. Kids don't really know what's in them, or how much they're capable of doing. They need to understand the concept of desire. They need to: a) focus on the objective; b) gather an inner intent to achieve that objective; c) reach down for all they have; and d) hurl themselves into action. They need to understand that their intent is the key. They don't have to believe they can push around every opponent; they just have to intend to and then commit to that intent. Talk to them about desire; get them to talk about it among themselves.

2. It's just roughhousing. Football is socially acceptable roughhousing; and it's great fun! It's quite helpful and very positive for kids to look at it that way. (See figure 1-2.) Football is a chance to go out on the field for a couple of hours and romp and tumble.

1-2. **ROUGHHOUSING**

It's about being king of the mountain—good, old-fashioned roughhousing.

It is better perceived as being "king of the mountain" type fun, instead of being about hostility. It's really not about violence or anger, as some coaches unfortunately teach kids. It's not about "going out there and hurting somebody," as some insensitive coaches yell (although, in their defense, they usually don't really mean it and are trying to fire a player up). It's just good, clean roughhousing. Help a player understand the difference, particularly if his nature is not to be aggressive. You don't want to change his nature, and you certainly don't want to make him violent. Teach him that it is possible to reach down within himself and bring forth a toughness, a sense of personal strength, an indomitable pride, and an intensity of spirit.

Many kids shrink from violent talk, so discuss the matter in a straightforward way, especially with players who are hesitant or struggling. Tell them that football is about roughhousing, pride, and teamwork. Yes, he needs to hit hard. Yes, he must concentrate and be explosive. But it's not about meanness. Channel his perception and energy in a positive way, and he will respond as if a weight has been lifted from him. He will begin to look forward to the next opportunity with a fresh, new purpose.

Another tip: Some coaches fail to understand that kids may be reluctant to deliver a hard jolt against a friend or schoolmate. Discuss this with the kids to help them understand that it's not personal. They are not out to injure or hurt each other. They should expect to be hit hard, and should encourage each other to go for it. They're a team!

3. Players are well protected. Many kids have a basic fear of getting hurt that limits their aggressiveness. Fear is usually the greatest obstacle in sports for young athletes. But since the physical protection football players have is excellent, they can and should rely upon it.

Players need to understand they are very well protected. Football equipment today is very good. Helmets have a special, scientifically developed lining that protects the head. The knees, hips, ribs, thighs, shoulders, and elbows are safely padded. (See figure 1-3 on page 8.) Weakness at the ankle, wrist, shin, or neck can be further protected with tape, wraps, or a collar. Neck collars are not mandatory, but I recommend parents buy one if it's not issued with the gear. My point is that the kids are *very* well protected. A player needs to understand how well protected he is, since the understanding will lessen his reluctance to really drive or slam into an opponent. Kids don't weigh very much in the youth leagues, especially in the first several years, and they usually don't have enough strength or size to give a really crunching blow, especially on the line of scrimmage. Injury is much less likely than in later years. You will occasionally see a hard hit, usually in an open field from a player with a head of steam, but you won't see it very often.

1-3. **REQUIRED PROTECTIVE EQUIPMENT**

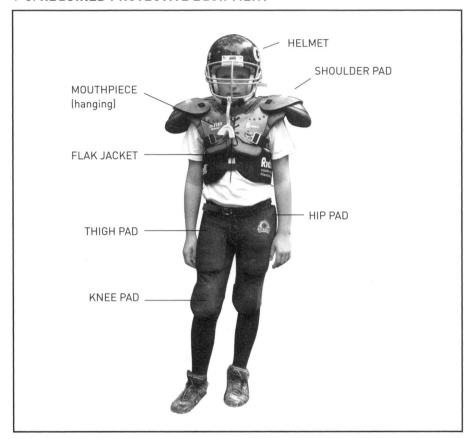

HELMET

SHOULDER PAD

MOUTHPIECE
(hanging)

FLAK JACKET

HIP PAD

THIGH PAD

KNEE PAD

The protection is quite thorough. Neck collars, elbow and forearm pads, and shin guards are not mandatory, but I advise parents to get them.

I've coached and played a lot of sports, and frankly, I've not seen more injuries in football than, for instance, in soccer or basketball. I believe there are two reasons for this: one is the protective gear, and the other is the more rugged conditioning that regularly occurs in football. Discuss this information with your players.

There is a great drill for blocking practice that I call Unirail. (See figure 1-4 on page 9.) Kids straddle a blocking pad one-on-one and block each other. They must stay straddled over the pad. This is a great drill for bringing out the fire in a kid. If a player doesn't hit hard, have him do it over. Tell him to hit as hard as he can. After that, ask if he got hurt, and when he says no, then ask why isn't he generally hitting as hard?

Run the play again, and keep repeating the question. After a while he'll get the point. It simply doesn't hurt. The sense of abandon you seek in him rests partially on his understanding that injury is not likely.

4. It's just for a few seconds. This is a very important motivational concept, especially for a marginal player, or a player up against a stronger opponent. The key is to understand that most running plays last just a few seconds. Players don't need to overcome their opponent forever, they just need to give it their all for a few seconds. Pop the player as hard as you can and drive for three or four hard steps. If playing defense, jolt the blocker hard and then shed him. A stronger opponent may eventually gain the upper hand, but for the first few seconds, a good pop and charge will slow down almost anyone. Of course, some plays last longer and the drive must be sustained for the whole play, but for the most part, just a few seconds of very hard effort are all that's needed.

What a player does in the first second or two determines how successful his play will be. Football essentially comes down to one-on-one competition. On any given play, most players on the field are locked in combat with a single opponent. Double-teaming and other maneuvers can require contact with several opponents, but most play is one-on-one. On the line of scrimmage, it's often against the same opponent for much of the game. Making the first move a quick, low, hard, driving jolt is the key to deciding how that one-on-one challenge will turn out.

1-4. UNIRAIL

This is a great drill for one-on-one coaching to build confidence and desire.

01

Sometimes the opponent is stronger, but sometimes he may be weaker. Usually coaches spot a mismatch and will stay away from plays directed to that position or double-team a strong player. But no matter how strong the opponent is, if a player does his best, especially for the first few seconds of each play, he will at least slow his opponent down. It's okay not to be able to succeed in every play. But it's never okay to give up. Maybe another teammate will be able to open a bigger hole if your kid is able to just hang in there. Even if he's getting beat again and again, he can't quit. He has to give it his best and find a weakness in his opponent by mixing up his approach and trying different things. A good opponent may play well, but there is great pride in knowing that you did your best and, by hanging tough, prevented the good player from completely getting his way. It's also consoling for youngsters to know that they are not expected to do what they can't; they are only expected to do their best and to not quit. More often than not, with increased desire alone, they can find a way to overcome the obstacle. Of course, we teach kids to play the entire play, but I find it helpful for them to focus on the first few seconds, and most often, that's all they need.

5. Win your personal game. Point out that desire is the determination to overcome your opponent. When that happens in a given play, there is a personal victory. Sure, it's a team sport, but winning your own battle is all that the individual can control, and even just a few such victories can lead to team success on offense or defense. A player won't win his own battle every time, but he can try, and he should feel good when he does win. Many times, the battle will be a draw. Sometimes the player will find himself on his butt, but seek the victories, and draw from them. And if the opponent is bigger and stronger, then any victory against him is big. Players should welcome such a match-up, since it gives them a chance to bring forth great courage and hidden strength.

6. Show you are interested. You can't make a kid do something well if he doesn't want to do it to begin with, but you can make him *want* to do it. You have to show the kid you care about him and are interested in his success. When a player feels you care about him, he will trust you and will want to do what you ask. If you are confident he can do it, he will begin to want to live up to your expectations.

7. Develop confidence. Confidence is a most elusive quality. Football is a sport that builds it. The coaches yell and bark a lot, kind of like the military atmosphere, but the idea is to get the kids to wake up. Most kids will get yelled at and will initially be upset by it. Parents will be worried by it and begin to feel protective. The coach is usually just trying to motivate the player, to toughen him up, to prepare him, and to get him excited enough to put a hard hit on someone. Unless the coach goes overboard by humiliating a player, the kids will get over it quickly and usually try a bit harder. Players often are surprised by what they can really do when they get their desire up. Sure, some coaches overdo it, and there are certainly problems if a hostile coach arouses the wrong feelings, but usually it's for the better. Once a kid sees what he can do, he'll keep on doing it. The coach is trying to get him to the point of giving himself a chance.

The antagonist of confidence is fear. Let's face it, we've all experienced it. Some people live with it daily. It's part of life. The ability to overcome or transcend fear is one of the keys to survival and, ultimately, to happiness. Each player has his own fears, and football can help bring him to terms with some of them.

A kid naturally worries about trying something new—will he be good enough, will he be able to take it? He finds himself flat on his back a few times; the coach yells; he is embarrassed. He gets back up. He keeps going. In a few weeks, he makes a big play and he starts to realize that much of the problem was just his own fear and self-doubt. He learns that he can overcome these insecurities with determination, hard work, and perseverance. He has found life's greatest friend … confidence. I've seen football lead to this, and it's a good thing.

Affirmations can help a kid give all he has to each play. "You can do it!" "I know you can do it!" "Hit with confidence." "Jolt him good." If the coach doesn't have confidence that a kid can get it done, the kid won't find it on his own. Tell him it's there for him, he can do it.

8. Play until the whistle blows. While it's important to focus on the first few seconds of the play, obviously players need to be in there for the entire down. Often, a kid stops moving when the play goes to the opposite side of the field. Nothing looks worse to the coach than a player standing still and watching the action. The player must continue until the whistle blows. He should run toward the play and stay busy and animated—do anything except stand and watch. This attitude helps keep his desire up. Sometimes, the play will reverse back toward him, so his continued effort can be quite important to the team.

02 THE GAME OF FOOTBALL: HISTORY AND RULES OF PLAY

Football is an intensely physical game in which two teams try to forcibly advance a ball against each other into the opponent's goal area. It is played on a field that is 100 yards long and about 53 yards (160 feet) wide. The field is marked off every 10 yards by a line from the goal line (or zero-yard line) on one end. These lines are numbered up to the 50-yard line across the center of the field, and down again to zero on the goal line at the other end. There is a 10-yard deep *end zone* at each end of the field. (See figure 2-1 on page 13.)

The main idea is for one team's offense to carry the ball into the opponent's end zone, scoring a touchdown, worth six points. The other team's defense tries to stop the offense by tackling the ball carrier and bringing him to the ground. So, each team advances toward *the other team's* goal with the ball, and then defends *their own* goal when the opponent has the ball. The offense has four chances, called *downs*, to move the ball 10 yards. If unsuccessful, the offense must relinquish possession. If successful, they receive another four downs to try to go another 10 yards.

HISTORY

In 1823, a student at Rugby School in England picked up the ball during a soccer match and ran with it. Players liked the idea, and so the game aptly called *rugby* evolved from soccer. Rugby football was played in America and Canada in the mid-1800s. The famous Rutgers-Princeton game in 1869, often credited as being the first intercollegiate football game, was, in reality, more of a cross between a rugby and a soccer game. The Ivy League schools, including Yale, Harvard, and Columbia, continued to experiment with combined running and kicking forms of the game. In 1879, Walter Camp, a player and coach at Yale University, developed what would become the basis of modern American football.

2-1. DIMENSIONS OF A FOOTBALL FIELD

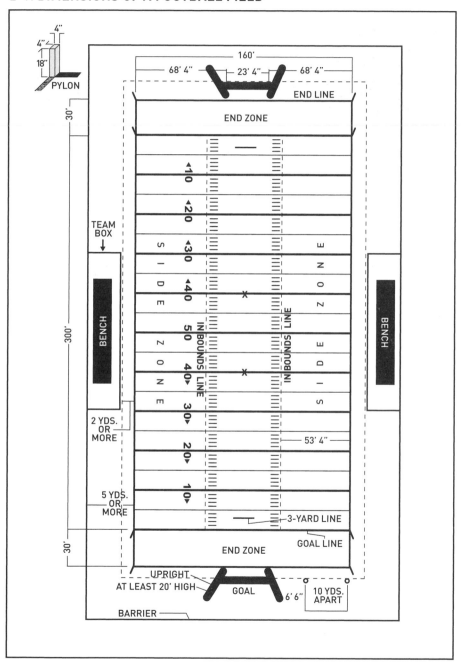

By 1900, the sport had widespread interest, and towns formed clubs and even began to pay some athletes to play for them. But the game became notorious for its violence and injuries, even deaths. President Teddy Roosevelt pushed for safer rules of play, and a national association, the forerunner of the National Collegiate Athletic Association (NCAA), was founded in 1906. While college ball dominated the early 1900s, professional ball continued to gain support. In 1922, the National Football League was formed. It rapidly gained broad public support. By the 1960s, collegiate and professional football rivaled baseball as America's top spectator sport.

THE CONCEPT OF DOWNS

One of the toughest things for people to understand about football is the concept of *downs*. I'll deal with it in depth here, but will also remind newcomers to the game that it will get much clearer after observing a few games.

Play begins after a coin toss to determine which team receives possession of the ball first. The opposing team kicks the ball from a kicking tee on its own 40-yard line. The receiving team catches the ball and tries to advance it toward the other team's goal. Once the receiver is *tackled*, or brought to the ground, the ball is placed on the ground at the point where it was when the ball carrier's forward progress was stopped. The nose of the ball then creates an imaginary line, extending from the ball to each sideline, called the *line of scrimmage*. Teams line up on opposite sides of this line, and the team with possession must advance the ball at least 10 yards from that line in four attempts. If they succeed, they get four more attempts to go another 10 yards from the point of the most recent tackle, and so forth. There is a 10-yard chain with a flagpole on each end on the sideline, usually manned by volunteers, that is used to measure the distance the team needs to advance.

Each attempt, or play, is called a *down*. Therefore, *first down and ten* means that the next play is the first of the four attempts and that all 10 yards still need to be covered. Similarly, *third down and two* means that this is the third attempt in the series of four downs and that 2 yards are still needed to make the 10 yards. If the offense gains more than 2 yards on the next play, then the team maintains possession. They are awarded another first down, and it starts all over again: They get four more attempts to advance another 10 yards. (The next play is called first and ten again.) Note that a team does not need to use all four plays to advance 10 yards. For instance, if the team passes for 20 yards on the first down, then it's a first down again at the new spot.

This can be difficult for the beginner. Let's try once more. Suppose my son's team receives possession on a kickoff and they begin on their own 20-yard line. To make a touchdown, they need to cover 80 yards and get into the other team's end zone. However, the rules of football require that the team only needs to worry about 10 yards at a time. My son's team has the first of four chances to move the ball the 10 yards, or in other words, to get it to the 30-yard line. We call that *first down and ten*. If they advance to the 30-yard line in four plays, they keep possession of the ball and get four more chances to go another 10 yards.

Okay, let's take it step-by-step starting back at the 20-yard line. Let's say our fullback carries the ball forward for 3 yards. The next play is referred to as *second down and seven* because it is the second try and they still need to move the ball 7 yards to reach the 30-yard line. Then let's say that a pass play gains 5 more yards. Now it's *third down and two* since the ball is on the 28-yard line after two attempts. Then my son catches a 9-yard pass. (Why not? It's my book!) Now the ball is on the 37-yard line. Since the team passed the 30-yard line as originally required, they now have another first down. The ball is on the 37-yard line and they have four tries to get it to the 47-yard line.

Now suppose my son had dropped the ball rather than catching that 9-yard pass. Then, it would be *fourth down and two* back on the 28-yard line. The team has one more chance, and if they fail, the other team gets the ball right there. Usually, when a team is near their own goal line on a fourth down, they choose to *punt* (kick) the ball to the other team so the opponents will have to go farther for a score. A good punt in youth ball will move the line of scrimmage 25 to 30 yards. That is why most teams punt on the fourth down, especially when on their own half of the field.

RUNNING A PLAY

Each team has eleven players on the field. The team with possession of the ball is called the *offense* and must have at least seven of their eleven players spread along the line of scrimmage. (See figure 2-2 on page 16.) These seven players are *linemen*, since they line up on the line of scrimmage. Their job is mainly to block the defenders on the other side of the line, and to prevent them from getting to and tackling the player with the ball. On offense, this leaves the quarterback and three players who are running backs or wide receivers. The player in the center of the line, who is called the *center*, hikes the ball back to the quarterback. (The ball is handed or *snapped* to the quarterback from between the center's legs.) The ball may be advanced by running it forward or by passing it to a receiver. In youth ball,

2-2. **THE LINE OF SCRIMMAGE**

Two teams line up on either side of the ball. One team tries to advance the ball, the other tries to stop them from doing so.

a play is over when a ball carrier's knee touches the ground, when a pass is not caught, or when the ball is run out-of-bounds.

After the ball is hiked to the quarterback, he usually hands it off to a running back, whose job is to advance the ball forward by running toward the goal line. Or, the quarterback could pass the ball to a receiver, who catches it and then tries to advance farther. The quarterback may pass forward or sideways, but he must be behind the line of scrimmage when passing forward.

The other team's defense is trying to tackle the ball carrier and to prevent a pass by batting the ball away. The blockers try to interfere with the tacklers. The offense may push with the hands but cannot grab or hold the defense. The defense is free to move as they please just prior to the snap, and they may shift around to confuse the blockers. After the snap, they may freely shove or throw blockers to one side with the hands. The use of the hands by the defense against a blocker is virtually unlimited, although the defense cannot hold, with the hands, a potential receiver from advancing downfield.

SCORING

A *touchdown*, worth six points, occurs when a team carries the ball across the goal line of the opposing team or catches a pass in the end zone. Scoring a touchdown also allows the team to attempt a *point after touchdown*. They can either kick the ball through the uprights of the goalpost for one point, or execute a running or passing play to get the ball across the goal line from a certain distance, worth two points. Professional football adopted the two-point conversion in 1994. In youth ball, the scoring is often reversed at the youngest levels. Since kicked points are more difficult for young kids, two points are awarded for a kick, and running the ball across the goal line is worth one point.

Another way to score is to place kick the ball between the goalposts and above the crossbar of the goal. This is called a *field goal* and scores three points. It usually occurs when the team with the ball faces a fourth down and the ball is within 30 yards of the end zone. If the coach feels that the odds are against getting another first down, he may try for a field goal. This rarely happens at the pre-high-school level of play since place kicking skills are generally poor.

A defensive team scores two points on a *safety* if they tackle a ball carrier in his own end zone. This often happens when the line of scrimmage is only a few yards from the offense's own end zone, and the quarterback is tackled trying to throw a pass.

After a total of forty minutes of play (forty-eight in high school and sixty in professional football), the team with the most points wins.

MAJOR RULES AND INFRACTIONS

Upon a violation of a football rule, a penalty is indicated by a referee throwing a flag. If the play has begun, it continues until the ball is down. Then, the referee explains the infraction and the team captain (usually upon a signal from the coach) can accept or decline the penalty. (A coach may decline a penalty if his team actually gained more of an advantage from the play than would be gained from penalty yards. A penalty may be declined, for instance, if it would be fourth down for the offending team and possession would change.) Penalties may be 5, 10, or 15 yards and are applied by moving the ball that distance against the team that committed the infraction, that is, in the opposite direction they are trying to go.

As a general rule, actions that are intended to hurt or maim are considered to be serious infractions. These include spearing with the helmet, punching the head with a fist or forearm, grabbing a facemask (the part of the helmet in front of the face), kicking or tripping, or jumping onto a pile of players. These actions can lead to a 15-yard *unsportsmanlike conduct* penalty or even an ejection from the game.

There are many rules in football so I will only review the main ones. To get all of the details, you should obtain a copy of the rules from the National Federation of State High School Associations, Box 361246, Indianapolis, Indiana, 46236 (www.nfhs.org). For college rules, write to the National Collegiate Athletic Association (NCAA) at P.O. Box 6222, Indianapolis, Indiana, 46206 (www.NCAA.org). These rules are generally similar to the rules used by youth football teams, including Pop Warner (the Pop Warner rule books are available to participating coaches).

My objective here is to discuss the major rules so that they make sense to you, particularly if you are a parent and not a coach. I may omit certain nuances in an ef-

02

fort to promote your general understanding. I advise you to get a copy of the actual rules for technical precision; the rules are worded quite technically in order to cover all possible scenarios that could occur. Coaches will need to read them carefully. Much more detail regarding some rules can be found in the glossary at the end of this book.

Offsides. This infraction occurs quite frequently. The term *offsides* covers several violations associated with players' actions at the moment of the snap. Basically, it prohibits an offensive player from crossing the line of scrimmage before the ball is snapped, and it results in a 5-yard penalty to the offending team. The rules also require offensive linemen to be motionless, in a ready or set position (i.e., hands on or near the ground) for a full second before the snap of the ball. Once in the set position, an interior lineman may not move his hands or head or make any other sudden movement or he will be charged with a *false start* and a 5-yard penalty. (See figure 2-3.) The purpose for this rule is to protect the defense from being "pulled" across the line of scrimmage by the movement of a lineman, since any offensive motion on the line ordinarily signals that the play has begun. If an offensive lineman jerks, a defender will charge forward. Defenders are taught to move as soon as a lineman moves. Therefore, the offensive linemen cannot move until the ball is snapped. Another purpose of this rule is to make sure that the offensive player does not get more of an advantage than he already has since he knows when the ball will be hiked. He

2-3. **OFFSIDES**

Note that the ball has not been hiked and the right tackle has moved into his man—a common foul.

cannot cross the line until the ball is hiked. What usually happens in youth football is that a kid forgets the cadence number for the hike and leaves on "one" when the ball is not hiked until "two."

The center, or snapper, may move the ball to get a grip on it, but he may not pick it up, stand it up, or jerk his head or shoulder. The running backs must also be set for a full second before the ball is snapped, although *one* of them may be in motion sideways or backward as the ball is snapped. Any other offensive back who is not set for the full second before the snap, or who is moving forward as the ball is snapped, is said to be in *illegal motion*. These infractions receive a 5-yard penalty.

Encroachment. This infraction is another form of *offsides*. Since it is usually committed by a defender, it is generally considered the defensive version of the offsides penalty. However, it pertains to all players. Picture an imaginary band the length of the football, from tip to tip, crossing the width of the field between the two teams. This is called the neutral zone. No player except the center can have any part of his body in, on, or over this neutral zone before the ball is snapped. In college and pro ball, if a defender crosses this zone but returns to his side without body contact before the ball is snapped, he is okay. However, in youth ball, once the center has grasped the ball, it's an offsides penalty as soon as the *neutral zone* is crossed. (See figure 2-4.)

2-4. **ENCROACHMENT**

The defensive tackle has stepped into the neutral zone before the ball is snapped and is guilty of encroachment.

Once the offensive interior linemen (the center, guard, and tackle) get into a set position, they must remain frozen before the snap. However, the defense can move around as much as they want, as long as they do not encroach on the neutral zone. As noted, the center—the snapper—may have his head or hand in the neutral zone, but not beyond it. The idea is to separate everyone by at least the length of the ball before each play. Encroachment carries a 5-yard penalty.

Pass interference. There are not many passing plays in football at the beginner levels. When the ball is passed, players cannot impede or restrict another player from catching the football once it is in the air, whether they are on offense or on defense. If the penalty is against the defense, it's a first down at the spot where the foul occurred (in college football, it's 15 yards from the previous spot or previous line of scrimmage). If the penalty is against the offense, it's 10 yards from the previous spot or line of scrimmage. If the infraction occurred before the pass is thrown, a similar penalty, such as *holding* or *illegal contact* is called. If defensive pass interference is called in the end zone, the ball is placed on the 1-yard line.

Facemask. If a player accidentally places his hand on or grabs an opponent's facemask during a play, the penalty is 5 yards. It is a 15-yard penalty if the player grabs the facemask intentionally or uses the facemask to pull the player to the ground. Often the violation is unintentional, and it is not usually seen by the officials unless it occurs against the ball carrier. (See figure 2-5.)

2-5. **A FACEMASK VIOLATION**

It is a 5-yard penalty when, as here, the hand gets into the facemask. It's a 15-yard penalty if the player grabs and pulls the facemask.

Roughing the passer/kicker. If a player makes hard contact upon a passer after the pass is thrown and the contact was reasonably avoidable, or makes any hard hit on a punter or place-kicker after a kick, there is a penalty of 15 yards.

Holding. Teams are often called for holding during a game. Holding is called against any player (but most often against an offensive lineman) who uses his hands or arms to hook, lock, clamp, grasp, encircle, or hold any opponent (other than the runner) in an effort to restrain him. (See figure 2-6 A, B.) Holding carries a 10-yard penalty. It can take the momentum out of an offensive drive.

Illegal blocking. Most youth football rules require that a player cannot block an opponent below the waist or *clip* him. *Clipping*, carrying a 15-yard penalty, is to block below the waist *and* from behind, except in the *free-blocking zone* (4 yards laterally and 3 yards deep from the ball). (See figure 2-7 on page 22.) Ordinarily, football rules allow such low blocks in this zone, but some youth rules at the very youngest levels emphatically disallow it even in the free-blocking zone for reasons of safety. Blocking in the back above the waist away from the neutral zone is also an illegal block, and it carries a 10-yard penalty.

Legal blocking occurs when clenched hands are in advance of the elbows but not extended more than 45 degrees from the body. If extended, the hands must be open and in front of the blocker's and opponent's frames. If the blocker makes initial legal contact above the waist and in front of the opponent and then either slides down below the waist or the opponent turns and continuous contact is made with his back, the block is legal.

2-6. HOLDING

A: A clear hold on the defensive player in white, as he is grabbed in an effort to prevent his open tackle—a costly 10-yard penalty.

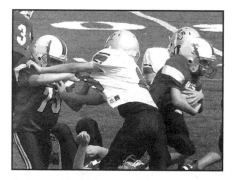

B: A more classic hold, grabbing the jersey to hold a defender back from making a tackle.

2-7. FREE BLOCKING ZONE

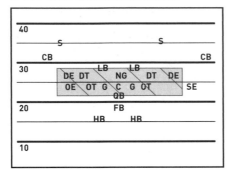

The free-blocking zone (shaded) is an area 8 yards wide by 6 yards deep, centered on the ball.

POP WARNER FOOTBALL/AMERICAN YOUTH FOOTBALL

Chances are most kids will play Pop Warner or American Youth Football, the two largest national football associations dedicated to youth football (although there are other youth football organizations as well). Both associations have similar rules. Pop Warner sorts out kids nicely according to weight and age groups with an eye to ensuring equality. Figure 2-8 on page 23 is a schematic showing the various groupings for Pop Warner. The American Youth Football weight matrix allows players to be heavier in each age grouping. A child's age on July 31 is his age for the season. Most leagues play the Pee Wee, Junior Midget, and Midget groupings. "Older/lighter" means, for example, that a fifteen-year-old who weighs less than 130 pounds can play Midget-level ball, even though this is usually for eleven to fourteen year olds up to 150 pounds. Every player must play at least eight to twelve scrimmage plays per game, depending on age. Most games will have forty to fifty plays in all. A kicked point after touchdown is worth two points while a pass or run into the end zone after a touchdown is only worth one point. Games are played for four ten-minute periods. The rules are strongly formulated to avoid running up the score between the teams; once a large lead is built up, starters cannot take the field until the score differential is reduced. Other than that, the rules are similar to high-school rules.

FLAG FOOTBALL FOR BEGINNERS

In 1983, as a result of increasing demand, Pop Warner instituted flag football. It was in response to leagues with few resources that needed to avoid the more expensive equipment required for tackle football. It also offered younger kids the opportunity to play, and the entry age was lowered from seven to five years of age. While flag foot-

2-8. AGE AND WEIGHT STRUCTURE—TACKLE FOOTBALL

Age/Weight Division	Age	Certification Weight Range
TINY-MITE	5–6–7	35–75 lbs
(older/lighter)	N/A	N/A
MITEY-MITE	7–8–9	45–90 lbs
(older/lighter)	N/A	N/A
JUNIOR PEE WEE	8–9–10	55–100 lbs
(older/ligher)	11	55–80 lbs
PEE WEE	9–10–11	70–115 lbs
(older/lighter)	12	70–95 lbs
JUNIOR MIDGET	10–11–12	80–130 lbs
(older/lighter)	13	80–110 lbs
MIDGET	11–12–13–14	95–150 lbs
(older/lighter)	15	95–130 lbs
JUNIOR BANTAM	12–13–14	115–165 lbs
(older/lighter)	15	115–145 lbs
UNLIMITED	12–13–14–15	160+ lbs
(older/lighter)	N/A	N/A
BANTAM	13–14–15	130–175 lbs
(older/lighter)	16	130–160 lbs

02

ball programs are offered in four age divisions from five to sixteen years of age, the predominant use is for the very young, ages five to seven.

I recall that skeptics worried that the kids were too young at five or six to play the game. They also had concerns about possible head injuries, since the kids don't wear helmets and are running into each other. Finally, they said that since the kids would be taught to use only the hands, the adjustment to tackle football would be very difficult. In tackle football, the shoulder is the more dominant body part, and kids must use the shoulder, more than the hands, to tackle and block. Just watch a flag game and you will see that these fears are not justified and are overridden by the great experience on the field. The kids love it, and the parents love it. It's a great Sunday afternoon of good, ol' football.

The game is quite simple. The rules are similar to tackle football in most respects. However, kids wear a belt with two flags attached at the hips by Velcro. The

2-9. **FLAG FOOTBALL UNIFORM**

Players each wear a belt with Velcro-attached flags, and they must also have a mouthpiece (here, it's in his hand) and rubber cleats.

only other equipment required is a mouthpiece and rubber cleats. (See figure 2-9.) Kids play on a shortened football field, usually 60 yards long and 30 to 40 yards wide, and the games are usually twenty-five minute running halves. They use an intermediate-sized ball. There are eight players on a side, with free substitution on a dead ball.

An important distinction is that blockers must keep their hands and forearms out in front of their torso. Defensive players similarly must use the hands or forearms to push blockers away. No punching or jolting movements with the hands are allowed. No shoulder blocking. No stiff-arming (running with the arm extended outward, palm flexed so the fingers are up). The idea is to keep the game safe. In some leagues, blocking is not allowed at all.

Many leagues do not punt or kick off, but just start play on the offense's 10- or 15-yard line, 40 to 45 yards from the goal (or end zone). A runner is tackled when one of his flags is removed by an opponent. Teams are allowe d four downs to cross midfield, and another four thereafter to score; otherwise, possession changes. Some

24

2-10. **FLAG FOOTBALL**

Flag football is great fun on a Sunday for the whole family.

leagues allow punts, while others just restart on the 10- or 15-yard line, as noted earlier. To promote the passing game, most leagues adopt a rule requiring the defense to count to three (in some leagues it's a five-count) upon a passing play before crossing the line of scrimmage. They can cross the line of scrimmage, however, as soon as the quarterback hands off the ball to a runner. Usually, quarterbacks are not allowed to run with the ball. (Coaches can use the playbook in chapter five and modify the plays for flag football.) The most effective plays are sweeps, off-tackle plays, and reverses. Short passes work well also. It's great game for beginners. (See figure 2-10.) And if the emphasis is kept on fun, kids will enjoy it and learn a lot.

03

FIELD POSITIONS

WHAT POSITION SHOULD A KID PLAY?

Well, that's up to the coach. During the first few practices, a coach usually asks kids what positions they want to play, but ultimately the coach decides who plays where. The first *wind sprints*, (30- to 40-yard dashes) tell the coach where the team's speed is, and speed is the primary determinant separating backs and linemen. Usually, the coach has certain things he is looking for: size, hustle, speed, strength, and coachability. Often, he must assign a person to a certain position because there is no one else on the team who can play that position. Remember, football is a team sport, and every player must play where he is needed most.

In general, the fastest kids play in the *backfield* on both offense and defense. This is the area more than 5 yards from the line of scrimmage—the open space where speed is essential. The biggest, most heavily built kids usually play on the *line*. Aggressive kids who combine speed, strength, and agility play *linebacker*. Inside linebackers play near the center, and outside linebackers play farther out, by the ends. Taller kids who have some quickness play *end*—offensive end if they can catch and block, defensive end if they can make tackles. In fact, if any kid has aggressiveness and can produce tackles, the coach will find him a place somewhere on *defense*. Big, strong, slower kids play *offensive line*, and the largest kids in this group play *tackle*. (See figure 3-1 on page 27.)

The *quarterback* is the kid who has intelligence, poise, speed, a strong arm, and the ability to complete passes. He must be able to receive snaps, remember complex plays (not just regarding his role, but everyone else's, too), and hand off the ball securely.

Sometimes it does not seem fair who gets to play where. But a coach's main motivation is to succeed, and he will generally put kids where they fit best. A kid's attitude plays a large role, too. The kid who has a bad attitude, who is oversensitive,

3-1. **FIELD POSITIONS**

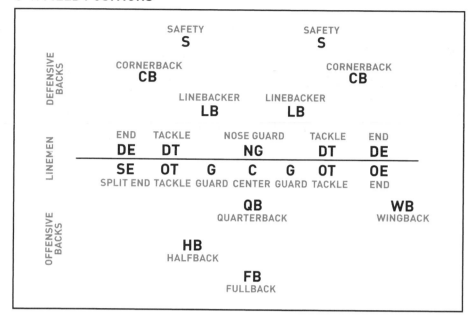

or who demonstrates any sort of problem will tend to be passed over for an equally talented player with a better attitude. This goes for the allocation of playing time also. A negative attitude is costly.

I believe football is generally good for a kid with a poor attitude. Most sports quickly teach kids the price they pay for acting up, so they have a chance to deal with it. They want to play, so they try to change. Hopefully, they get a coach who helps them control their emotions, instead of one who makes it worse. I've seen coaches get pretty nasty with a kid who just needs a friend; some even drive the kid away from the game. We'll talk more about this in chapter seven, but kids are all different, and a good coach will account for those differences. I'm not saying to play favorites or to treat some kids better than others. Different kids respond to different approaches, and a good coach will figure out how to reach a kid with potential.

At some point, a player may get upset because his visions of scoring touchdowns have been dashed by an assignment to another position. Don't exacerbate his frustration. He'll get over it. He will learn how to have just as much fun tackling ball carriers or opening holes for them. Remind him that a coach has to play the fastest players at running back, that it's a team sport, and that he should try to be as good as he can at the assigned position. I also recommend talking to the team early in the season about what it takes to play various positions, and how each position is important. No individual statistics are kept, and every touchdown belongs to the whole team. It's also a good idea to allow some kids to try out various positions during practice scrimmages. Many coaches have been surprised at how a kid can excel at a new position when given a chance.

There is a position on the field for each child. Let's talk a bit more about each position. Please keep in mind that the basic skills for these will be covered in chapter four. The idea here is to focus more on the nature of each position and what the player needs to understand about it.

OFFENSIVE POSITIONS

OFFENSIVE LINEMEN
Center

The center is just that—he plays the center of the line. His role is to snap the ball to the quarterback, avoid a fumble, and still make a good block against his man. He has to have perfect timing synchronized to the quarterback's cadence, or his hike will be late and his team will be offsides. He must remember the cadence and the *count*, the number upon which the ball must be hiked.

The center has a slightly different stance from the rest of the line. His feet are spread wide and his hips must be high to allow for easy passage of the ball between his legs. The legs are positioned fairly evenly and must not move backward upon the snap to avoid tripping the quarterback. His weight is moderately forward on the ball. Some kids need both hands on the snap, although one hand is better, freeing up the other to deal with the oncoming opponent. The center's head must be up and may be in, but not beyond, the neutral zone, that area between the front and rear of the ball. The arm is extended, and he turns and tilts the ball as is needed for a good snap. (See figure 3-2 A, B, C on page 29.)

The center must snap the ball quickly at the precise time. A very quick, firm snap is essential. The elbow bends slightly and he releases the ball to the quarterback. Of course, a center practices the snap thousands of times. Usually, the quarterback wants the ball on a certain angle to fit his hand, with the laces hitting his hand by the fingertips. Different quarterbacks receive the snap a bit differently, and their hands may be in a slightly different position—this is why fumbles often occur in a game when quarterbacks are switched. The correct angle of the snap must be worked out. The center's hand also

3-2. **THE CENTER**

A: Center is a tough position, and it takes a special kid to play center. His form here is excellent.

B: The ball is held so the the laces are exposed to the left of the hand.

C: The snap is high so the quarterback can safely grasp the ball.

needs to be well forward on the top of the ball so that his hand is on the opposite side of the ball from the quarterback's hands upon transfer.

The center may step forward as he snaps. It may be a simultaneous motion, stepping and snapping, although it's important not to disturb the ball as it is transferred.

This is true only for the center; other linemen can't begin to move forward until the ball is already in motion. The center's first step must be very quick and should be straight forward, not to the side, and he should step with the foot closest to the side where the play will go. (See chapter four for center snapping on punts and kicks.)

On most plays, the center will be required to block a *nose guard*, a defenseman who sets up in position directly facing the center (right on his nose) or an interior defensive guard if the defense chooses to position their players in the gaps, or spaces between offensive linemen. If the running play is up the middle, a guard will often assist the center in the block, thus *double-teaming* the nose guard to ensure he cannot make an easy tackle. The main job of any lineman is to *open a hole* in the line, that is, remove or push a defenseman from his position so a space is created for the ball carrier to safely run through. The center's job is to give the nose guard a good pop, try to get in under his shoulders and stand him up, and then allow the guard to push him away from the runner. If the center is individually blocking the nose guard, usually on an off-tackle or an end run, the center must try to get to the runner's side of the nose guard and ensure that he does not penetrate the line of scrimmage; he should try to slow down any sideways pursuit.

The center needs strength, not speed, but most particularly needs to be able to complete the snap under pressure and still give a jolt to the onrushing nose guard.

Guards

On each side of the center are the two offensive guards. Offensive linemen all need strong legs since their principal job is to drive opponents away from their positions. However, guards also need to be quick. While most blocking for beginners is straight ahead and upon the opponent directly across the line of scrimmage, guards eventually will be asked to *pull out*. In this move, the guard turns upon the snap and runs laterally along the line of scrimmage to trap an opponent who is charging across the line by hitting that player from the side. It's an effective blocking style since the opponent often does not see the pulling guard until too late, and a block from the side will often succeed. Guards also pull and lead the runner through an off-tackle hole (the space between the tackle and the end). We will discuss pulling skills in more detail in chapter four; the basic idea is to take a short step with the foot on the side of the pull, and push off with the down hand and with the foot opposite the direction of the pull. Bending his knees, the guard stays low, runs close to the line of scrimmage, and then strongly jolts the opponent.

3-3. **DOUBLE-TEAMING**

The guard (#57) and the tackle double-team the defensive tackle.

Guards need strength, as do all interior linemen, but also need quickness, and will rely upon various kinds of blocking techniques more than other linemen. They block one-on-one against defensive linemen, as do other linemen, but they do much more. Guards often will double-team a lineman or be called upon to *cross block* a nose guard or defensive tackle. (See figure 3-3.) We'll discuss such blocks more fully in chapter four. Also, guards are most often called upon to block linebackers, the toughest defenders on the field. Guards must use their quickness against an equally quick and usually larger opponent, and somehow stay between the linebacker and the ball carrier. Blocking linebackers is clearly the toughest job for the offensive guard.

Tackles

Moving from center outward along the line of scrimmage, next to the guards are the two offensive tackles. (I played this position in high school.) Tackles are usually the biggest and strongest offensive linemen when weight restrictions are removed for older kids. They generally block straight forward into a defensive tackle who is just as big, or bigger, than they are. Sometimes tackles are called upon to block a linebacker or a defensive end, or if the play goes to the opposite side of the field from them, they go downfield to block a defensive back. They rarely pull, although it does occur occasionally on a wide running play. Size and strength are both needed since this position involves a one-on-one, straight-ahead, short-distance power struggle between two big players. (See figure 3-4 on page 32.)

3-4. **THE OFFENSIVE TACKLE**

Here, #70 has good position on the defensive end, having turned him from the ball, opening a good hole.

Offensive running plays, as will be discussed later, usually are *dives* up the middle, *slants* off-tackle (outside the tackle, between the tackle and the end), or *end runs* (wide sweeps around the end). On dives up the middle, the tackle shoots forward a step and stays between his opponent and the ball, trying to impede his opponent's lateral movement. On wide plays, the defender has the outside advantage (usually lining up on the outside shoulder of the tackle), and so the block is much tougher. On sweeps, the idea is to delay the opponent from penetrating, and also to delay or impede the opponent's lateral pursuit. Off-tackle plays, however, require the best effort. The opponent must be driven out of the off-tackle hole and turned away. This is the toughest job for the tackle. Often, on an off-tackle run, the guard and tackle, or end and tackle, will do a *cross block*, that is, cross over and block each other's opponent. One player, usually the inside lineman, steps out first and blocks the other player's man, then the second lineman crosses over and blocks the first lineman's man.

ENDS
Tight Ends

The offensive ends line up, you guessed it, at either end of the offensive line. If he is lined up close to the tackle, he is a tight end; if split a few yards out, he is a split end. The tight end needs to be tall, since height helps when receiving passes. He also needs to be quick enough to catch short passes. As a lineman, he must be strong enough to block the defensive end and even the big defensive tackle when called upon to do so. Since the tight end is close to the interior linemen, he, in effect, acts as another blocking lineman. He spends most of his time blocking, and these skills must be worked on even more than receiving. Great tight ends are great blockers. I played offensive end in my earliest years (before I got so big that I could block better than I could catch and was moved to tackle). I enjoyed this position because I got a chance to catch passes.

A very effective pass is a quick *slant*, where the tight end dashes out, slanting directly behind the defensive line toward the middle of the line, and the quarterback, who doesn't even drop back, fires the ball to him from close range. It's a tough pass to catch since it must be thrown very hard and quickly, but it's quite effective. Often, a defensive end tries to jam the tight end—just give him a shot to slow him down—and of course this can eliminate the effectiveness of a quick slant pass.

Very often, the tight end is called upon to block downfield. This skill comes very slowly in youth football, and does not seem to be emphasized by coaches. These blocks are always difficult since defensive backs are very quick and agile and can use their hands fully. Usually, the best that can be hoped for is for the tight end to slow down the defensive end a step, but this is often enough. Kids don't usually regard downfield blocking as important, yet more than any other block, it can lead to a touchdown. Remind your players that they must play until the whistle blows, and to always find someone to block.

Split End/Wide Receiver

Split ends and wide receivers are primarily pass receivers. Depending on the offensive formation used and the play called, there could be none, one, or two of these players on the field. A split end lines up about 2 yards from the tackle and will either run a pass pattern or execute a downfield block. The split end's stance is similar to that of the other linemen. He is usually a yard or so outside the offensive tackle.

Wide receivers line up very wide, at least 3 to 4 yards from the closest lineman, to ensure that they draw only one-on-one defensive coverage. If they line up wide, but a yard behind the line of scrimmage, they are called a flankerback. They need great speed, agility, leaping ability, quickness to fake a defender, and courage to concentrate on receiving a pass, knowing that as soon as they do, they will be hit quite hard. (See chapter four on receiving.) At the pre-high-school level, especially at the younger levels, football is not much of a passing game since there are few *completions* (passes caught by the offense) and usually as many *interceptions* (passes caught by the defense). However, the wide receiver is still out there waiting for his day to see that long pass spiraling toward him over the clamor below. This is one of the truly great moments in all of football. Fans hush and hold their breath. Things seem momentarily suspended as the ball is high in the air. No downfield contact is allowed while the ball is in flight, and the fleet-footed players are running at full throttle to snatch the ball from the air. Long pass receptions are clearly the most popular plays in the pros, and they are the most beautiful to behold. Wide receivers are the great athletes of football and rival quarterbacks for the glory of the game.

BACKS
Halfbacks

Halfbacks are the fastest kids on the offense and can run hard and hold on to the ball even after a solid tackle. They do most of the ball carrying for that reason. They line up behind the quarterback, ready to receive a handoff or block for another back. They also can go out for a pass, but their primary job is to advance the ball. They usually run off-tackle or wide around the end, leaving the short-yardage, straight-forward dives, for the stronger fullback. We'll cover the stance, the pivot, and ball carrying skills in detail in chapter four. The keys to a good, quick start are the quick snap of the head and shoulder, the sharp pivot into the direction of the play, and the step-out. It is also essential not to tip off the defenders by looking or leaning in the intended direction before the hike. The linebackers are carefully scanning the halfbacks' faces and stances for any clue as to the play.

Halfbacks must move with explosive quickness in an endeavor to outrun the field, especially on wide sweeps or end runs. (See figure 3-5 on page 35.) The moment of decision occurs when a defender approaches. Try to run away from him? Or dance and spin around in an effort to fake him? Or cut back to the inside and find a hole? Or perhaps lower the shoulder and ram forward, happy to settle for a few extra yards? Cutting back and those fancy steps could spring long yardage, but also can lose a yard or two. The running-hard approach is more conservative and usually gains a few yards. The halfback needs to learn what he is most successful at doing, and what's needed at the moment. Remember, a few yards are very valuable pieces of territory. They can be the difference between a first down and losing possession. I generally like to see kids run hard and get the few extra yards, but the real key is for a player to follow his instincts.

3-5. **THE HALFBACK**

The sweep is the most effective play in youth football if you have a speedy halfback who can run away from the defense. Here, the ball carrier runs past the defense.

Fullbacks

Fullbacks are the biggest and strongest of the running backs. They run the ball up the middle, usually on a straight dive play to one side of the center. They are expected to pick up a couple of yards regularly in short-yardage situations. They run low and hard, with their heads up. They are expected to hit the hole very hard. It may not be a big hole, so they must capitalize on any advantage their blockers give them. Fullbacks don't dance much; they run hard and low and need a lot of momentum. Fullbacks rely on their momentum to push the tackler back so they can fall forward, gaining every extra inch possible. Short, quick steps and pumping legs can propel a fullback as he falls for an extra yard or so. Usually, both hands are pressed over the ball, holding it firmly to the stomach. The distinction between a halfback and a fullback was best stated regarding old-timers and Hall of Famers Jimmy Brown and Jim Taylor. Brown, a halfback, would give you his leg and then take it away. Taylor, a fullback, would give you his leg and then ram it through your chest.

Fullbacks do a lot of blocking. They often lead the halfbacks on sweeps, off-tackle runs, or even on some halfback dives. They block for the quarterback on passing plays. They must take fake handoffs and convincingly draw linebackers to them as they pretend they have the ball.

35

Quarterback

The quarterback is a gifted athlete who is able to handle the ball securely, is agile in traffic, and is able to pass accurately, even if he is on the run. He has good vision and a strong arm. He must know what everyone does on every play, and therefore he needs to be smart. The quarterback must be a natural leader, able to motivate the players and to control his own intensity. He must take charge on the field and gain the respect of his teammates. His footwork must be precise. Fakes must be very convincing; good habits are necessary here. He must execute secure handoffs, and, of course, his passes must be accurate. The quarterback must learn when to throw, when and how to throw the ball away or out of bounds, and when to take a *sack* (being tackled while still in possession of the ball). He needs to understand when to *scramble* (run away from a tackler) to avoid a loss of yardage. When a play breaks up, or someone misses an assignment, the quarterback must be able to react, improvise, and go with the flow of the play. Chapter four will cover the fundamental basics of passing and handoffs.

The worst thing for a quarterback is to fumble constantly, and it happens frequently at the youth level. Fumbles are killers to an offense trying to move the ball downfield and are most painful to coaches when they result not from contact but from bad ball handling. Repeated practice taking snaps is mandatory. A quarterback must take the snap securely *before* he pulls back from the center. Prematurely pulling back from snaps, perhaps from a slightly late snap, causes many fumbles. There is no better way to take the steam out of a drive than to drop the snap. To prevent a dropped snap, the quarterback must get low, bend the knees, and get the hands under the center's crotch far enough to secure the snap.

Sharp, quick moves by the quarterback are necessary so the backs can run the ball through the hole created by the blockers before it closes. I often hear parents screaming for blocking when, in fact, the blockers did their job, and delay in the backfield was the real problem.

The quarterback lives in the eye of a swirling, grunting, clawing hurricane. He must stay poised. He can't worry about whether players are doing their jobs, and he must go about his job with calmness and precision. Jerky, panicky moves lead to fumbles or cause a quarterback to trip or collide with his own players. He must also keep the offense coordinated and stay within the twenty-five seconds allotted to get a new play going after each down. He must know his personnel and try to find out where the defense is mismatched and where it is weak. When all else fails, he should rely on his most consistent teammates.

DEFENSIVE LINEMEN
Nose Guard/Inside Guard

This position, a single position head-on to the offensive center in a five-man defensive line, or two positions lined up facing the center-guard gaps in a six-man defensive line, requires a special kind of kid. Action comes from all sides very quickly. The most valuable piece of turf in the game is usually the one the nose guard stands upon. So the main objective of the nose guard is to hold his ground.

His stance is a bit more solid and balanced that that of his defensive teammates on the line. (See figure 3-6.) The best stance is a four-point stance to ensure a low, well-braced charge. The worst thing for a nose guard to do is to stand up too quickly because, especially if he is double-teamed, he will be easy to move away. His charge should include a good shoulder jolt. Then he must crawl and scrape his way forward, always low enough that he cannot be driven away. The nose guard can *submarine* (dive low into the gap) and scramble back to his feet. Another good move is to dive over a low-charging center. But, most often, the nose guard executes the defensive skills typical of all defensive linemen, they just do so a bit lower. Even if he is on his hands and knees, he is at least blocking the hole, slowing down the runner, and piling up bodies in the middle.

When double-teamed, the nose guard hits one blocker with his shoulder and fights off the other with his hands, turning his body sideways to claw his way through the

3-6. **THE NOSE GUARD**

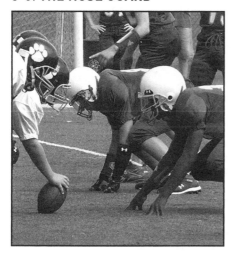

The toughest position in football is the nose guard. He lines up head-to-head with the center. The nose guard here is in excellent form: low, poised, even with the nose of the ball.

seam between two blockers. Remember, this is not a wrestling match; the idea is to shed the blockers. A major fault with defensive linemen (tackles and ends) is that they tend to focus too much on wrestling with their opponents. As explained chapter four, the idea is to hit the defender hard, to neutralize his charge, and then to shed him quickly. The nose guard must get rid of the blocker as fast as possible, not wrestle with him. It's not a contest to see who is stronger, but a contest to get away from the blocker.

Defensive Tackles

The foundation of the defense is at the tackle position. The nose guard is expected to ward off the runners and to at least clog up the running lanes in his middle area; however, the tackle is expected to earn his name by tackling, tackling, tackling. The two defensive tackles are usually the biggest and strongest kids on the team and are also aggressive enough to hold ground, penetrate, and bring the ball carrier down. As with the nose guard, the tackle must hold his ground. Tackles are responsible for tackling the ball carrier on off-tackle plays. The main area they are responsible for is head-on. The nose guard is often double-teamed, so the dive play up the middle must be expected; but keep in mind this play is the linebacker's main responsibility. At the least, tacklers must hold their ground, and they should penetrate if possible. On short yardage, they hold and protect inside; on long yardage, they penetrate, looking to rush a passing quarterback and get a possible *sack* (tackling the quarterback before he gets rid of the ball). They are always under control and prepared for the possible block from the side by a guard looking to trap him.

Tackles usually line up on the outside shoulder of the offensive tackle on a five-man line. The inside foot is back and it steps first, while the front foot drives inside toward the pressure. Remember, as noted previously, defenders don't wrestle. Defensive tackles shed the blocker and drive a shoulder into the ball carrier. They should avoid arm tackles since those are weak. However, if off-balance, tackles should grab onto whatever is available.

Most kids don't fully understand the effect a good, hard jolt has on their opponents. They use more of a *shiver*, just hitting the blocker at the base of the shoulder pads and driving upward with their outstretched hands. Sometimes it looks like they are playing patty-cake. (See figure 3-7 on page 39.) A shiver move works best on the tight ends, but on a lineman down in the set position, a defensive tackle is much better off giving a good shoulder shot and *then* using the forearm and hands to shed the blocker and hunt for the ball. Keep reminding players to, "Hit, shed, and hunt."

3-7. **THE DEFENSIVE TACKLE**

Avoid the tendency to use the hands to just push. Instead, come in low with a jolt and then shed the opponent.

Defensive Ends

Defensive ends are usually tall with good upper-body strength to hold off blockers. There are two positioned at either end of the defensive line. Usually, a defensive end has to ward off multiple blockers before he gets through to the running back on an end run.

The defensive end is responsible for the outside, that is, for the wide running plays. He should cross the line of scrimmage for several steps, then turn and force the play to the inside where there is more help and less running room. A defensive end is often blocked by an offensive end, by a pulling guard, or by a fullback on an off-tackle play. His job is to keep those plays to the inside and to force the action even farther inside. One of my most vivid football memories is seeing the running back behind three blockers all heading toward me. The job is the keep the play inside, where there should be some defensive help.

On a pass play, the defensive end is a key pass rusher, always looking to tackle the passer before releasing a pass, and he has a great angle to crash on the quarterback.

The defensive end stands up on the line of scrimmage, arms at the side, crouched down a bit. He positions himself a bit outside the offensive end, or a yard or so off-

3-8. **THE DEFENSIVE END**

The defensive end is in good position—slight crouch, hands down and out, outside foot back.

tackle if the offensive end is split. (See figure 3-8.) The inside foot is back and steps forward first. The end should quickly penetrate several yards and then turn to face the play. He should guard against the sweep, but also look to crash in on the off-tackle play or pursue a run to the other side. He must not be too quick to pursue, but look first for a possible reverse play before he leaves the area. The *shiver charge* described earlier is usually the most effective weapon for the defensive end to use to ward off blockers.

The defensive end, as is the case with all linemen, must stay under control. He should not leave his feet if at all possible—particularly during a pass rush—since a faked pass can take him out of the action and thus open up the outside area to a scrambling quarterback. The biggest mistake that defensive ends make is to get faked inside, believing that the offense is running the ball inside or up the middle when the apparent handoff was just a fake. It happened to me, and I remember the terrible feeling as I watched the real ball carrier sweep untouched around my end on his way to making big yardage. The end must hold the outside under all circumstances.

DEFENSIVE BACKS
Linebackers

Linebackers are usually the toughest kids on the field. Depending upon the defense used, there are usually two to four on the field. They are the heart of the defense. Their job is to figure out where the ball is going and to stop it. While a defensive lineman is expected to get blocked or double-teamed, a linebacker has fewer excuses. He stands freely, with

3-9. **THE LINEBACKERS**

The linebackers are the key to the defense. They are the second line of defense, just behind the linemen, and they quickly penetrate holes from their standing position.

a few yards of space to react to the action. He must have a lot of upper-body strength to throw off blockers, the agility to avoid them if possible, and a pounding aggressiveness.

Linebackers have a crouched, balanced stance, weight forward on the front of the feet, hands down and palms out, a yard or so behind the line of scrimmage. (See figure 3-9.) They scan the offense for clues as to where the play will go. The offensive guards are the best clues, since on the snap they usually move in the same direction as the ball. (I will review the keys to reading offensive motion in chapter five.) The linebacker must meet an approaching blocker with great strength and vigor. He must drive his forearm or straight arm into the blocker's upper body, right under the shoulder pads (without grabbing the pads) to neutralize the blocker, and then quickly shed him. He must directly address the head-on blocker, give a blow, shed, sidestep, and then hunt for the ball carrier. The linebacker closest to the runner usually goes directly into the hole being opened by the offensive line.

During a pass play, the outside linebacker angles and looks to the *flat* (sideline area) on his side to pick up any receiver heading there and covers him. While outside linebackers have responsibility for the flat, inside linebackers mainly are concerned with defending against the short pass over the middle or a quarterback scramble.

SECONDARY
Defensive Backs/Deep Backs/Safeties/Cornerbacks

The deep backs, safeties, and cornerbacks are fast, tough kids who are the last line of defense. They must tackle any ball carrier that gets past the defensive linemen and

3-10. **THE DEFENSIVE BACKS**

These players need it all: speed, aggressiveness, endurance, and ferocity.

linebackers. Most important, they must catch the breakaway runner and prevent a score. They must be in great shape and have good endurance, because in this position, they run a lot. Whenever the ball goes to the opposite side, they must take a *pursuit* angle, heading to a point where they can intercept the runner. (See figure 3-10.) The biggest mistake a defensive back can make is to fail to pursue a breakaway runner and cut him off. The concept for the secondary is always to rotate into pursuit; that is, when they see a runner breaking away for a large gain on the other side of the field, they first back up and then circle toward the other side of the field, picking an intercept angle with the runner.

Defensive backs must make aggressive tackles but always be under control. They are often the last defender, so a missed tackle will cost the team a high price. They should edge to the outside of the runner if possible and force him inside, where there may be more defensive help.

In a passing situation, the deep backs *always* look to intercept passes. They must expect and anticipate an interception, and always be trying to catch the ball. They cannot let a receiver get behind them, that is, between them and the end zone. They should never let the receiver get too close to them, because they always need some room to react to a change of speed or direction.

SPECIALTY POSITIONS

There are several other positions that specialize in very specific skills: punters, place kickers, punt and kickoff returners, long snappers, and place-kick holders, as well as those who play on special teams performing the blocking or tackling required of the given team. We will discuss specialty skills further in chapter four. Obviously, if a boy can punt or place kick, he will be a valuable player since these skills are rare for young players. Punt- or kickoff-return players are sure-handed receivers who have very good open field running ability and are able to avoid onrushing tacklers in open space. Long snappers need to be able to consistently deliver a spiral ball hiked from between their legs accurately to the waiting hands of a player situated 4 to 8 yards behind them, depending on the play. Place-kick holders also must be sure handed since they must catch a long snap and very quickly place the ball in position for a place kick. These players are often quarterbacks who are sure-handed and able to pass the ball if called upon to do so if a fake place kick is called.

03

04 FUNDAMENTAL SKILLS

Certain basic skills must be learned and then executed on every play. Blocking and tackling are probably the most important, since on any given play most of the twenty-two players on the field are doing either one or the other. Each player must learn how to block or how to tackle, and if he learns both, he can play on both offense and defense. Passing, running, receiving, and pass defense are essential football skills. There are also specialty skills such as punting, place-kicking, and snapping the ball. *Special teams* is the term used to describe the eleven players designated to perform specialty functions.

As mentioned in chapter one, the desire to overcome the opponent is of primary importance. However, poor skills can greatly reduce the effectiveness of individual effort. An informed coach or parent can be most helpful in this respect, particularly with regard to proper form. Help each boy with the details of technique *before* he develops bad habits that will take years to change.

Often, with twenty to thirty players on the field at practice, the coach may not notice flaws in a player's form, or he may not communicate clearly to each child the technique and concept behind the correct form for various positions. This is where a parent can help. Focus on your child's form at practices or at a game. Scrutinize his stance, the height of his attack, whether his legs are digging forward, where his hands and forearms are positioned, how long his effort is sustained, and other areas covered in this chapter. I have also included some drills you can use to work on form.

Frankly, I think videotapes of practices, scrimmages, or games are very effective tools for teaching. I don't think they are used very often below high-school level. Yet, I believe videotaping players is an excellent method for reviewing form and execution. I've used it, and it works well. Zoom in as close as possible. Then, when you view the tape later, look at my checklist of techniques in chapter ten. Review and discuss each one with your players. There may be no better coach than a player's own eyes. Give him the chance to see his errors and allow him to correct them himself.

BLOCKING

Blocking is the attempt to prevent a defensive player from tackling the ball carrier, preferably by removing the player from the ball carrier's path, but at the very least by interfering with his ability to tackle. Many plays in youth football don't succeed because someone forgot to block (or didn't know who to block). Or a player may miss a block because of poor form or not trying hard enough. Blocking is done by everyone on the offense, but it is the primary job of the offensive linemen, especially the five interior linemen. They are the unsung heroes of the game. Even a defensive lineman will hear his name on the loudspeaker when he makes a tackle, but it's rare that an interior lineman gets public credit for a great block that led to a touchdown. These players must learn to play just for the personal satisfaction of being part of a team and of overcoming their opponents. Sure, there is less glory, but the true fan of football knows that all positions on the field are of equal importance. Offensive backs (including quarterbacks) know that they live or die based on the performance of their linemen. Linemen do a tough job, and they have to love it. I know—I was one of them when I played.

Early in the season, a player may go home a bit disappointed when he finds out that he has been assigned to a line position. He may have started the season with dreams of being a quarterback or linebacker, then he finds he will play a position he rarely thinks about. Chances are it's because of insufficient speed. If this happens to your child, be supportive. Remind him that he is part of a team and should focus on being as good as he can be wherever he is needed. And point out all of the important jobs he has in his position.

Often, at the youngest ages, the most yardage is gained by a speedster just running wide around the whole pack, since blocking up the middle is often ineffective. The kids are still learning blocking techniques. Usually, the best athletes play in the backfield or on defense, so the offensive line gets second best. Also, the defense often shifts and uses different formations or *stunts* (players switch upon the snap to penetrate through each other's areas). If you look at the interior linemen, you will often see kids standing straight up, seemingly leaning on or pushing each other. (See figure 4-1 on page 46.) With such poor blocking form, a hole for the running back is often not formed. As the boys mature, their blocking is much improved, and dive plays up the middle become more effective.

4-1. BLOCKING

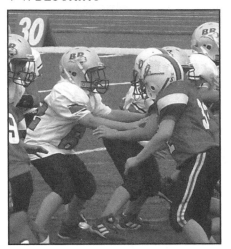

A typical scene in youth football: Linemen standing up and merely pushing each other.

FIVE PARTS OF THE BLOCKING STANCE

The purpose of the correct stance is to give the blocker a good start. Each part of the stance is designed to increase a player's potential to overcome his opponent. A lineman must be able to get low enough so he can make it under the opponent's center of force, which is under his shoulders, and yet still have enough power and balance to jolt the opponent, raise him, and sustain the block. It's a tall order, and good form helps.

1. Ready position. A lineman begins in the *down* or *ready* position. He sets his legs a few feet back from the line of scrimmage and squats. The legs are spread about as wide as the outside of the shoulders, with one foot back a few inches. Hands are on the knees, and the eyes are straight ahead. Upon command of the quarterback, the lineman snaps down sharply into the *set* stance (explained below), from which he begins the block. The ready position ensures that the snap movement into the set stance is smooth and deliberate. Once a lineman is in the set position, he cannot move again until the ball is snapped. Therefore, the movement into the set position must be exact. It is a twofold motion: The back foot drops back a few inches and the hand on that side drops to the ground into a three-point stance. Once his knuckles touch the dirt, a player cannot lift them again without incurring a penalty, so it helps to move to the set position from a consistent posture every time, and that's the ready position. (See figure 4-2 A on page 48.)

2. Set position: feet apart and balanced. In the set stance, a lineman's feet should be spread *at least* shoulder-width apart. If his feet are too close together, his opponent will be able to shove him to one side. Action in the middle of the line is heavy and a player can easily be hit from the side and knocked off-balance. The toes may be pointed slightly outward for power and balance. However, with legs spread, the blocker has greater lateral balance. The weight mainly rests on the front or balls of the feet. The toes of the back foot are even with, or a bit behind, the heel of the front foot, although this can vary according to the player's size and sense of comfort. Taller players often set the back foot farther back than do shorter players. The goal is to have short, choppy steps. Starting with the feet not too staggered helps balance. The back foot should not be adjusted once in the set position since any movement can be viewed as intention to draw the defense offsides. (See figure 4-2 B on page 48.)

The front foot is the power foot, and as the back foot steps forward with the snap of the ball, the front foot drives into the strength and thrust of the opponent. The back foot is brought forward for balance and to sustain the block. Theoretically, the back foot should be the inside foot (closest to the center of the line), so the power thrust toward the inside with the outside foot is maximized, but it is also important to be comfortable and feel balanced. Kids usually drop the right foot back no matter which side of the line they're on. A good drill is to have a player squat with his feet in the set position and roll his body weight on them. He can find the foot position that seems to give the best balance for his body frame. This drill also strengthens the lower legs.

3. Three-point stance, weight moderately forward. Lineman use a three-point stance to block. The hand on the same side as the back foot snaps down to a point on the line just inside of the back foot and just forward of the shoulder. The weight is rolled forward; the knuckles are down and the thumb is back. Some kids like to balance on their fingertips, but the knuckles give much more stability. The weight should be moderately forward on the hand, just enough so that the player would fall forward slowly if this hand were suddenly removed. With sufficient body weight forward, the player can get a fast start and build momentum quickly. However, with too much weight forward, the player cannot react sharply to defensive movement, particularly stunts, and he cannot pull laterally if that is his assignment. The other forearm should rest comfortably on the thigh. However, don't forget that arm! It must be poised, fist clenched, ready to drive forward and up into the opponent's chest. The three-point stance is recommended over a four-point stance, especially for offensive linemen. It's very tough to pull, trap, cross block, or adjust to stunts from a four-point stance.

4-2. **READY AND SET POSITIONS**

A: The ready position is an interim position, getting ready for the set position. Two variations are shown here, one with forearms on thighs, and one with hands on the knees (though the hands should be closer to the knees).

B: Once set, the offensive lineman should not move.

C: Incorrect set position: Tail too high, head down, legs not bent enough, and they are too close together.

D: Incorrect position: Tail too low, weight back, and hand too far back.

4. Back straight, tail down. The purpose of the stance is to create a low, coiled position from which to launch the shoulder forward under the opponent's shoulder and to generate enough power to lift and thrust the opponent out of the way. If the back legs are not bent enough, then they are not coiled with maximum power. Furthermore, straight legs lift the tail up higher than the shoulders and detract from the forward thrust, wasting energy in a downward motion. Finally, it is hard to keep the head up if the tail is too high, and a lowered head limits vision. The tail should be even with the back, or even slightly lower, for maximum effect. However, if the legs are bent too far into a squat, the player loses time and effort to straighten out. The squat stance is often seen in youth football and should be corrected. (See figure 4-2 C, D.)

Another common problem with a young player is a rounded back. This happens when the legs are not bent enough or spread far enough apart. If the down hand is not out far enough in front of the shoulder, it can also result in a rounded back. In effect, the player is merely bending down from the waist. This is a very weak position, and it is dangerous since the head is also down too low. Make sure that the back is straight and parallel to the ground.

5. Neck bulled, eyes forward. Looking straight ahead is critical. The defense, especially the linebackers, are trained to look at the eyes of the offense for clues to where the play will go. Your player certainly does not want his opponent to know that he intends to block him. If anything, teach your players to look straight ahead or at someone they will *not* block. The element of surprise gives an important edge to the offense, so an offensive player must learn not to tip off the defense by looking at the person he will block, or by looking to where the ball will go. It is especially important not to lean in the intended direction of the play; even a slight lean will give important information to the defense. Scrutinize practice or game films for form defects or body signals that need to be corrected. A blocker should angle his thrust to the left or right depending on the path of the ball carrier, but he must not do this before the ball is snapped. A "poker face" is important, so discuss this with your player. Tell him to bull his neck, bracing it for contact, keep his head up and chin forward, and give away no clues.

If a player does not bull the neck and instead allows it to tilt or slant downward, two things can happen. First, he doesn't fully see the defender and can lose him or have him slide off more easily. Second, he may strain his neck upon contact. A blocker needs to develop the habit of bulling his neck on every play.

FIVE KEYS TO THE BLOCKING CHARGE

1. Explode with the snap of the ball. The most important moment in blocking is the first second after the ball is snapped. The offense knows exactly when the ball is to be snapped by the center to the quarterback, but the defense does not know it. The quarterback calls out a cadence of signals and ends with a series of sounds, such as "hike, hike, hike" or "hut-one, hut-two, hut-three." The quarterback has already told the players when they were in the huddle which of these numbers will signal the snap.

This is a valuable opportunity. It is the "edge" the offense has—the element of surprise. Coaches should not vary the count cadence too much, since kids forget the count frequently, but just the fact that the count can vary gives an advantage. The blocker can set his angle and charge forward before his opponent moves. He can strike with full momentum before the opponent has a chance to build up any momentum, . Therefore, a quick charge at the same instant as the snap can give the blocker a very powerful edge.

I don't think that the need for a very, very quick thrust at the moment of the snap is emphasized enough in youth football. You can correct this by talking about it. If a player understands the concept and the edge it provides, he will have discovered a powerful tool. I remember thinking about trying to hit my opponent across the line before he even moved a muscle. Tell your players to try it during practice. This approach will increase his quickness and add to the explosiveness of his initial contact. Even if the opponent is farther away, such as a linebacker or someone in the defensive backfield, a quick move is important. Quickness can be practiced. Look again at the discussion of desire in chapter one, and the notion that the first few seconds are so very important, since plays usually last just a few seconds. Players should thrust with both feet, giving the body forward momentum.

2. Stay low with legs wide and knees bent. The most common mistake young linemen make, especially at the beginner level, is to stand up as the ball is hiked. This reduces the power of the forward thrust and eliminates any chance of delivering a good, hard jolt to the opponent. The edge from knowing when the ball will be snapped is also lost, and the blocker becomes vulnerable. All he has is his strength, and the opponent now has an advantage since defenders can fully use their hands to shed and shove the blocker sideways. A lineman must stay low with the charge and keep his head up and knees driving forward to build maximum momentum.

4-3. **DRIVE BLOCK**

This is near perfect form for a drive block.

3. Raise forearms forward and elbows out for a shoulder jolt. The forearms are aimed for a point under the opponent's shoulders, rising forward in anticipation of contact, ready to slam into and raise the opponent's upper body upon contact. The elbows are initially spread outward to broaden the blocker's breadth as much as possible. This helps to hinder an opponent who tries to run to one side or the other. Youth coaches often teach beginners to *punch* the opponent with the hands thrust out, ramming into the chest with the palms, just under the shoulder pads, rising upward to raise the opponent's chest. This type of straight-ahead blocking is called a *drive block*. (See figure 4-3.) This is better for younger kids, who may have trouble sustaining a shoulder jolt and drive, but the stronger thrust is clearly made with the full force of the shoulder. The ramming shoulder is much more powerful than outstretched palms, so it's better to lift with a forearm thrust followed by a shoulder jolt. Coaches often give up on shoulder jolts and let the kids default to just shoving the defender away, but the correct way is to use the shoulder. Good form will get the shoulder into the opponent's body.

4. Angle, don't step, to the opponent's side. A common mistake blockers make is to initially step to one side, trying to cut off the opponent from the path of the ball carrier. It's a natural move, and I did it myself plenty of times to secure the angle I needed. However, it reduces the momentum of the forward thrust and also lessens the advantage obtained from knowing when the ball will be snapped. Overall, it takes away from the jolt that can be delivered. It's a trade-off. If I was stronger than my opponent, I preferred

51

to secure the lane and didn't need the jolt since I could still overpower him. But if he was good, then I had to rely more on quickness.

Generally, the charge should be straight forward, angled just enough for the blocker to get his head on the side of the opponent where the ball carrier will run. The objective is to give the maximum jolt, and then, after stunning the opponent, to turn and force him away from the play.

5. Detect and adjust for stunts. Again, if the charge is quick enough, a blocker can pop an opponent before he gets in gear. However, the blocker needs to be aware of stunts and adjust accordingly, particularly if the opponent is not close. If the opponent is slanting to one side, then the blocker must adjust his thrust. If the opponent is a linebacker, then his stunt may take him out of the play and another player will need to be blocked. Decisions must be made quickly, and the ability to adjust takes experience. It is important, however, to know which angle the opponent is taking, and to be generally aware of what other nearby defensive players are doing.

FIVE KEYS TO THE BLOCKING JOLT

If you haven't already noticed, I love the word *jolt*. It really captures the essence of what the blocker should try to do. Ask a player to think about what happens to him when he is jolted himself, how he feels stunned for a moment. Ask him how easy it would then be to move him around. This is how a blocker wants his opponent to feel, even if he is distracted for only a split second. A good jolt deflates the opponent's momentum and allows the blocker to stand him up and get deeper into his midsection. Furthermore, it distracts the tackler from finding the ball carrier, and, most important, it teaches him respect for his opponent and makes him more cautious during future plays.

1. Jolt hard and as low as possible. If the opponent is head-on or just to one side of the blocker, the jolt is the culmination of the charge. The basic idea is to slam a rising forearm and shoulder into the opponent as hard as possible. The blocker should be as low as possible and get under the opponent's shoulder. But in close quarters, with only a split second, he has to take what he can get. He shouldn't sacrifice the jolt for position. A good jolt is a powerful and effective weapon. He can smash the forearm and shoulder into the opponent, then worry about what to do next. The ideal is to hit the opponent's upper thigh and drive up into the midsection. But, whatever part of the opponent he hits—often it's the shoulder—the objective is to belt it hard. The concept is to view the shoulder as a battering ram or as a boxer's punch, and throw it hard into the opponent. If the opponent is farther away, the blocker has time to dip just before making contact. The dip is like a windup that loads more power, and it also serves to get the body a bit lower before the jolt.

2. Drive, don't lunge. The idea is to thrust and bring the back leg up. The initial charge is hard, but it is not a lunge. The knees straighten out upon contact. It's important to be under control so that the next move—a sustained block—can be carried out. The eyes must be open. The blocker must not turn his head away, for it is possible for the opponent to slide past him. The jolt occurs quickly, and a blocker needs to be under enough control to maintain balance and sustain contact with the defender.

3. Maintain balance. Often, blockers lunge too hard, or the defender's quick reaction causes a blocker to make contact off-center. Whatever happens, it is critical to keep the legs wide and regain balance by bringing the back leg forward and under the body. The eyes must be open to assist with balance. The blocker must feel the direction of the defenders rush and drive directly into it. At all costs, he must avoid losing balance and falling to the ground. It happens often, and a player can do little on the ground. If necessary, a block can be sustained by supporting the upper body with a hand on the ground. If the blocker does fall, he must keep blocking from the ground, sliding or crawling into the defender to try to interfere with the tackle in some way. Remind him never to stop trying.

4. Drive up into the opponent with short, choppy steps and turn him. Once the jolt is delivered, with the legs still wide, the blocker drives the defender back with short, quick, choppy steps. He maneuvers his body between the ball carrier and the defender, lifting the defender with the hands and forearms. He keeps up constant pressure to interfere with the tackle, trying to turn the defender away from the path of the ball carrier and then back to the line of scrimmage to prevent pursuit, and keeps his legs under his body as much as possible to avoid losing balance.

5. Use the hands, palms out, to shove the defender. One of the most common errors committed by an offensive lineman is holding. This penalty is called as often as offsides. A defender starts to get by a blocker and the blocker grabs him or wraps an arm around him. The blocker can use open hands, palms out, after delivering the jolt to push the defender, as long as his hands are extended and are out in front of the blocker's and opponent's frames. But he can't grab or hold any part of his opponent or his opponent's uniform with his hands or arms. Holding incurs a costly 10-yard penalty.

04

SPECIALTY BLOCKS

Angle, trap, or mousetrap blocks. It's a lot easier to block a player from the side than it is to block head on. The straight-ahead block, or drive block, often results in a stalemate at youth-level ball. The kids get their hands into each other and push, but little happens. *Angle blocking* is more effective, since a good jolt from the side will often move a defensive player. Blocking from the side avoids all of the opponent's thrust and momentum. Sometimes he doesn't see it coming and is fully exposed to a good jolt. The technique is to drive into or under the defender's near shoulder. The blocker's head is in the gap, between the opponent's linemen, hands pushing or punching at the defender's front and side.

In addition, *traps* are often set up. Traps are blocks that approach a defender from the side or a side angle, not head on. The simplest trap is a *cross block*, in which two blockers who are next to each other cross and block each other's man. Usually, the offensive tackle crosses in front of the offensive guard, blocking the nose guard or a linebacker; then the offensive guard traps, jolting the defensive tackle from the side as he crosses the line of scrimmage. The offensive tackle must move very quickly toward his man and get out of the guard's way, or a quick defensive tackle will penetrate to the ball carrier. The offensive guard pauses and then quickly pivots, charging with strength into the side of the onrushing defensive tackle. It works best when the defender has forward momentum, since the blocker can just "ride" him using his own momentum to push him out of the path of the ball. Sometimes, a tackle and an offensive end will cross block, with the end going first and the tackle then trapping the defensive end.

In another trap, a lineman *pulls*, that is, drives his body laterally instead of forward, turning and running sideways along the line of scrimmage to trap a player. Traps are effective because a defender is attacked from the side, and is thus more vulnerable. Usually a guard does the pulling, although occasionally a tackle pulls. Only good athletes should do any pulling on the line. When pulling, the blocker pushes to the side with his down hand (the hand touching the ground in the set position), pivots, and drives along the line of scrimmage with the outside foot, that is, the foot opposite the direction he is heading. The arms pump quickly to get up speed. He must stay close to the line of scrimmage, and with his eyes on the hip of the defender he is assigned to block, he should bend his knees and jolt the opponent. (See figure 4-4 on page 55.) If the pulling guard is to lead the play through a hole, he enters the hole, widens his legs, stays low, and blocks the first defender to come from the inside (usually a linebacker).

If a guard with his right foot back has to pull to the left, then his first step is obviously with the left foot, driving with the outside foot. The step is a short one, and it should be back a bit and not too close to the line of scrimmage.

Sometimes the defender senses that a trap is coming. He's coached to drop immediately to all fours, especially if he's a nose or inside defensive guard. This is done so the defender can still use his body to plug up the gap the runner is heading toward and also allow the defender a chance to drive himself into the runner, perhaps slowing him down, or even tackling him. If this occurs, the trapper must prepare to dig him out by driving into his side or shoulders (not with the helmet) and by trying to turn him or just lay upon him. (See figure 4-5 on page 56.) The blocker must always play the defender during a trap, timing the charge to the speed and height of the defender.

Downfield blocks. Quickness is key here. When blocking a player downfield, that is, more than 5 yards from scrimmage, the blocker must get to the opponent as quickly as possible. He must stay on his feet and must stay under control to make contact, since the defender has plenty of space to try to avoid contact with the blocker. Downfield blocking is the primary blocking style done by receivers during a running play, but it is also done a lot by linemen during runs to the opposite side of the line from them. They head across the downfield area on an angle, searching for a defensive back.

4-4. THE PULLING GUARD

Here, the guard (far left) pulls to the right to cross block the defensive end.

The blocker must know the path of the ball carrier. Often, a defensive back is approaching the ball carrier at an angle. The blocker's objective is to get his head between the defensive back and the ball carrier, and drive his opposite shoulder into the defender's midsection. In other words, if the runner is to the right and the defensive back is approaching from the left, the blocker steps in front of the defender with the right foot and drives into him with the left shoulder. Once the blocker makes contact, he rides the defender and simply interferes, slowing him down as much as possible.

When I played football, a well-timed *cross-body block* was the most effective downfield block. Here, the player pivots on one foot, lifts the other leg up and outward, and turns his body horizontally, balanced on the one leg, driving his hip into the opponent's midsection. He must make initial contact above the belt. This block is not often taught in youth football, perhaps for safety reasons and to avoid any possibility of blocking below the waist. However, it is effective since the horizontal body is so wide, and thus hard for the defender to avoid.

The *stalk* block is a very effective downfield block in which the blocker gets close to the defender, legs pumping, hands inside and clenched, stalking the defender's movement and trying stay in between him and the ball carrier. he must keep the helmet to the play-side of the defender, that is, the side the ball carrier is on. (See figure 4-6 on page 57.)

4-5. DIG HIM OUT

The defenseman has dropped to all fours so the blocker comes in low to dig him out.

Double-team blocks. These are very effective and necessary in youth ball, and are often used against a very strong defender. Two blockers simply drive their shoulders into either side of the opponent and drive him back. Another option is the *post and wheel*, in which one blocker hits straight-on and the other hits to one side, trying to turn the defender away. (See figure 4-7.)

Crackback blocks. This is a highly effective blocking technique in youth level play. A wide receiver, flanker, or split end, comes in (i.e., *cracks back*) toward the center to block a defensive end or linebacker. A crackback block must be carried out in the free blocking zone (see again figure 2-7). The player cannot make low contact from behind, or a clipping foul will be called. But, working as a trap, it can be very effective.

Pass blocks. Here, the blocker does not charge, but drops a step back and toward the middle and holds his ground. He keeps his hands in front of him with his legs churning, and his responsibility is to block the area in which he is standing. The blocker lets the defender come to him. (See figure 4-8 on page 58.) He looks to visually pick up any stunts, and he jolts the first defender to approach. The idea is to interfere with and stop any defender rushing to the passer, or at least to slow them down or turn them away. The best technique is to *shiver blow*: Drive both palms forward and up into the defender's shoulders, then recoil and shiver again. The blocker should stay

4-6. STALK BLOCK

Nice stalk here to the left: Hands are out and head is to the runner's side, stalking the defender.

4-7. POST AND WHEEL

One blocker (the post) hits from the front and the other wheels the tackler around from the side.

57

4-8. **PASS BLOCK**

Linemen engage defenders or drop back looking for someone coming in.

as low as possible to keep the defender's hands low and out of any passing lane. Pass blocking is much easier than other types of blocking, as long as the blocker keeps his balance, stays on his feet, and interferes with the pass rusher for as long as possible. The objective here is not to overcome the rusher; it is to slow him down and thus protect the passer.

Other Blockers

Our focus so far has been on blocking by linemen. Many of these techniques apply to blocking by running backs as well. They often find themselves facing a situation similar to that of a downfield blocker. On a sweep play, the blocking back needs to get outside the defender if he can. On a play to the right, he must get the right foot out in front of the defender and squeeze the left hand and elbow in front of him also. Then he simply drives into the defender with the left shoulder. This kind of open field block form is also useful for guards when they pull on an end, and it is similar to the downfield blocking form. If the play is designed to cut inside, then the blocker reverses and hits with the outside shoulder, driving the defender outside.

Blocking Assignments

Linemen in youth ball often don't fully understand the plays. If you use too many plays each game, the problem is compounded. The more they understand the plays—how the backs are lined up, what fakes the quarterback is making to try to get the defense off balance, what each running back is doing—the better they will be able to react to changes in the defense or defensive stunts. You *must* find out what defenses your opponents use and in what situations, and practice running your plays against these defenses before the game. (I'll discuss scouting in chapter seven.) You also need to spend time with your team, explaining the plays with a blackboard early in the season.

Coaches use various tips for kids who get confused and don't know what to do in a given situation. The best rule of thumb is to first go for the defender head-on. If that can't be done, go for the first player to the inside of the line, whether a defensive lineman or a linebacker. If there is no one head-on or inside, hit the nearest defender. Know where the ball carrier is headed, and get your head to the playside of the defender.

BLOCKING DRILLS

Form is where we start. Get the offensive linemen into two (or three) rows, with each row having five players (two tackles, two guards, and a center) in their regular positions. If there are any blank spots, that's okay. Each line should be 10 feet from the next.

1. "Down, set, hut" drill. Call out "Down!" and all players snap into the down (ready) position. Coaches walk among the players working on form. Then call out "Set!" and all players snap into a set position. Coaches again roam looking for form issues. All players should move as a unit, and coaches should note who is out of step with the others. Coach calls "Hut!" and players all take two to three steps as if blocking. Coaches review the intensity of the charging jolt, whether hands and forearms are rising, and if legs are driving.

2. Dummy drill. Players line up as above, except the two lines face each other. One line holds up dummy pads, and the other line charges into the dummies on *hut*. Instruct the line to provide mild resistance at first, then increase defensive resistance while requiring blockers to maintain form. Call for some cross blocks and pulling plays to practice form for those blocks.

3. Timing drill. Players line up as in the "down, set, hut" drill. Coach calls out a play and the count, as if he were a quarterback in a huddle, such as "I-147, on two." Then he calls out the cadence regularly used by the quarterback at the start of a play, such as "Down, green, 247, set, hut-1, hut-2, hut-3." The players snap into a ready position upon hearing the "down" command. Call out the play slowly and review any players in

04

59

incorrect posture. The color (here, I named green) is a pre-set signal that may change the play that would have been called in the huddle, and the 247 is the name of the play (so if the signal is that the color green changes the play, then 247 is the new play, any other color means we're doing the play called in the huddle, which was I-147). Upon the command "set" the players snap into the set position. Again, the coaches review form. When the coach says "hut-two" (the signal called in the huddle for the hike), the players charge into a blocking step. (They should take two steps in that direction, using the block they would make for their position.)

The idea is to get the *timing* of the charge down. Players should charge on the correct count with a strong driving movement, while coaches see if they know their plays. Do this a dozen times. Insist on proper form and proper timing. Change the *hut* number from one to two to three randomly to see who forgets and charges on the wrong number. Call the signal for a pass play and see if they snap into a pass block posture (step back, hands out, feet chopping up and down). If the play involves a pull, or cross block, check to see if it occurs properly. This drill is good practice for proper form, timing of the charge, remembering plays, changing plays, and remembering the count. Hand out laps or push-ups to offenders.

4. Blocking sleds. Sleds are metal structures with upright padded flexible sections simulating an opponent, all of which are attached to a moveable sled. Players block into the pads, allowing coaches to review form. They are also great for building leg strength and a good blocking jolt. Sleds come in different sizes, allowing from two to seven players to practice at a time. Make as much use of sleds as you can. Watch the impact players make on the sled, and refuse to accept anything less than their best efforts. Make a player repeat lunges into the sled until he hits it with abandon. This is where you can really bring out the "pop" in a player's jolt.

5. Unirail drill. This is described in chapter one on pages 8–9 and listed here as a reminder, it's a great drill. Kids straddle a blocking pad one-on-one and block each other. They must stay straddled over the pad. This is a great drill for bringing out the fire in a kid. If a player doesn't hit hard, have him do it over.

TACKLING

Defense is about tackling. I believe tackling best demonstrates the essence of football. The most tenacious kids on the team will play defense; they will do so because they make tackles. Tackles don't have to be pretty, they just need to stop the ball. Less aggressive kids can play the offensive line, but defensive play absolutely demands desire and the kid who loves the fray. Good tacklers are hard, tough kids.

Tackling is the act of stopping the forward progress of the ball by forcing the ball carrier to the ground. The object is to stop the ball cold, not even allowing the ball carrier to fall forward an inch. The ideal tackle hits the ball carrier hard enough to force him backward, preferably causing him to lose possession of the ball. A fine, crunching tackle always brings great praise from fans, coaches, and teammates.

Proper form for tackling comes naturally to an aggressive kid. His mind is focused on stopping the ball carrier, and anyone else is an obstacle to be overcome quickly. He claws and fights by or through the interference and comes in hard on the running back. There are, however, several concepts and techniques that the beginner should understand.

I will discuss defense in general and the play of individual defensive positions in chapter six.

FIVE KEYS OF THE DEFENSIVE LINE STANCE

Every single play in football begins with a proper stance. This holds true for each player—offensive and defensive linemen, backs, and receivers. Everyone should start each play with a proper stance. Tackling, therefore, also begins with a solid stance, especially for the down linemen. The worst thing for a defender to do (besides getting knocked to the ground) is to allow a blocker to get a shoulder into his belly. The defensive stance is less rigid than the offensive stance, since an offensive lineman cannot move once he is set. Defenders can adjust, stunt, or change the intended angle of thrust at any time, depending on the situation.

1. Choose a three- or four-point stance. The defensive lineman's stance when down in a set position is similar to the blocker's. Feet are wide and balanced, with one foot back a bit more than it would be in the offensive stance. This gives more push to the defensive charge. The weight is forward, *significantly* more forward than the blocker's, again to provide forward momentum. The back is straight, with the tail down and head up, looking at his opponent for clues to the play, and looking at the ball. (See figure 4-9 on page 62.) The defensive lineman must get as close as possible to, but not in, the neutral zone. It's optional whether one hand is down or both hands (in a four-point stance). Some coaches like the four-point stance since it gets the body lower and also gets the momentum forward more quickly. It's more important for a nose guard or the interior defensive guard on a six-man defensive line (we'll review formations later).

The three-point stance mounts less of a thrust but affords more mobility. A four-point stance may be used by shorter, quicker players who need more thrust but are agile enough to react as needed. If a four-point stance is used, the weight should be distributed evenly on all fours.

2. Stay as low as possible. The defensive lineman's shoulder should be even with or lower than the blocker's shoulder. The worst thing a defensive lineman can do is rise up too quickly and let the blocker give a blow to his midsection.

3. Put one foot back, preferably the inside foot. The down lineman, that is, a lineman in down or set position, can more squarely handle an outside blocker on a sweep or off-tackle run if he drives forward with his front or outside foot. So, therefore, it is better for the down lineman to keep his inside foot back. The ankles can be flared out for more power.

4. Keep eyes forward, searching for clues. Defensive linemen should check their opponent's eyes and look for any slight lean by the opponent. They look at the quarterback, running backs, and other linemen, trying to get a feel for the direction of the play. They should think about the down and the yardage, and whether a pass or a run is likely. Usually, teams won't run the same play twice, so a good defender tries to predict where they might choose to go next. Valuable clues can be gained. But a

4-9. **DEFENSIVE STANCE**

Defensive stance is low, similar to a blocker, but his weight is more forward for more thrust.

defensive lineman must not think so much that he forgets to watch the snap or fails to react to what actually occurs.

5. Stand in a crouch stance. Defensemen such as ends and linebackers stand in a crouch, knees slightly bent, inside foot forward, arms hanging to the side, hands waist high, palms out, and weight forward, balanced on the balls of the feet.

TOP FIVE TACKLING TECHNIQUES

I like linemen to think of themselves as ramming machines. The basic idea is to meet the blocker, neutralize his charge, and move into and against the blocker's pressure to find and stop the ball carrier. It is critical to keep these two concepts in mind: The tackler must hit the blocker to neutralize him, and then recover and shed the blocker.

Common errors are rising too soon to look for the ball carrier, or trying to shed the blocker by stepping around him without neutralizing the charge. A tackler must give the blocker a good jolt of his own. Keep repeating: Hit and hunt, shiver and shed, neutralize and move on. Let's go through the steps of tackling one by one.

1. Watch the snap and act quickly upon it. The defense is not allowed to be in or across the neutral zone when the ball is snapped. (Unlike professional football, defenders may not retreat back across the line before the ball is snapped if they make no contact.) Defenders must anticipate the snap of the ball and explode very quickly upon it. The first move in football is almost always the most important, and quickness is usually a part of most successful moves. The quarterback will try to pull linemen offsides by varying his cadence, and referees will usually allow it unless it is flagrant. So, while players must listen to the cadence and tense up near the time of the snap, they must focus on the *actual* snap of the ball. The offense knows the count. They have the clear advantage of surprise and can build up momentum behind their charge and jolt. The defender can compensate by using quickness to minimize the offensive momentum. (See figure 4-10 A, B on page 64.)

2. Neutralize the blocker's charge. There are basically two ways to do this: a shoulder charge or a shiver charge. A *shoulder charge* is used when the idea is to penetrate the offensive line. The defender jolts the shoulder against or under the blocker's shoulder just like in a block, simultaneously bringing up the forearms to lift the opponent, bringing up the back foot for balance, and driving through using short, choppy steps. He must always have his head up, looking for the flow of the play, that is, the general

4-10. **CHARGE**

A: This tackler has used quickness to penetrate the gap, slightly turning his shoulders to get through.

B: This tackler punches his hands into the blocker's chest to raise and jolt him.

movement of the the offense, and searching for the ball carrier. The key is to stop the blocker's charge and momentum and thus be in good shape to shed him. A shoulder charge can also be used when no penetration is desired, such as a short-yardage situation when the defense needs to protect territory. In this case, the defender focuses on neutralizing and then on *lifting* the blocker.

4-11. **SHIVER**

This defender neutralizes the blocker with a shiver, holds him at bay, and prepares to shed him.

The *shiver charge* is used to protect territory by neutralizing and holding the blocker at bay while looking for the ball. (See figure 4-11.) Defensive ends and linebackers use it most, but it can also be used by down linemen who want to mix up their approaches. The idea is to jam the opponent's shoulder pad with the palms in an upward direction using a stiff, straight-arm move, palms out, with both hands. The lineman keeps the opponent away until he spots the ball carrier and then sheds him. Again, neutralizing the blocker's charge head-on is preferable to trying to step around him, since such avoidance often exposes that player to an easy block from the side. Another common error is to rise to look for the ball before neutralizing the blocker.

Sometimes a neutralizing charge is not used, and a *submarine dive* is used instead. This is a knee-high dive between two opponents during which the defender uses his quickness to penetrate. The key is to bring the legs up very quickly and to do a push-up with the arms to regain a ready position after diving through the line. It works well against taller blockers or blockers who don't stay low. This move is used particularly by the nose guard to mix up his stunts and keep the blocker off-balance. However, a hard neutralizing charge is usually the best way to control the neutral zone and win ball games.

3. Stay under control. If no blocker shows up, there is no one to neutralize. When a defensive lineman doesn't get blocked immediately, chances are a player is pulling from the line and preparing to trap him from the side. Warning bells should go off! The defensive lineman should slow down, stay under control, drop to the ground, give the trap blocker a forearm or a shoulder, and hold fast to try to plug up the hole toward which the ball carrier is headed, i.e., stack things up. He can scratch and crawl on all fours toward the ball carrier, trying to slow him down or stop him. If he only plugs up the hole, he at least forces the runner to go around him—hopefully closer to another defender.

4. Recover and shed. When two onrushing opponents give each other a jolt, chances are the defender was hit harder due to the blocker's greater momentum. This is why the recovery must start simultaneously with the jolt. To recover, the defensive lineman brings the forearms up, lifts, and begins to push the opponent away. Then he drives forward with short, choppy steps. He looks for the ball and drives toward it. (See figure 4-12.)

5. Focus and wrap. Now it's showtime—it's between the tackler and the running back. Once a tackler has thrust the blocker to one side, he should drop down a bit to a low position, keep moving, and focus on the runner's belt. (See figure 4-13 A, B on page 67.) He spreads his feet, head up, and drives his shoulder low into the upper-leg area. This is not a lunge; the legs and hips are under him. He jolts with the shoulder, drives his hips forward, and clasps his arms tightly around the runner. He then lifts and drops him quickly, driving the legs and arching the body as needed. Tacklers should always be aware of the ball, and try to dislodge it without sacrificing the tackle.

The eight coaching keys for tackling are: 1) feet must be spread, 2) head is up, 3) shoulder slams into the thigh of the ball carrier, 4) hips stay in under the torso, 5) arms are clasped tightly, 6) then squeeze and lift the ball carrier, 7) drive the legs, and 8) drop him.

4-12. SHED

Having shed his blocker, #55 now seeks the runner.

4-13. **THE TACKLE**

 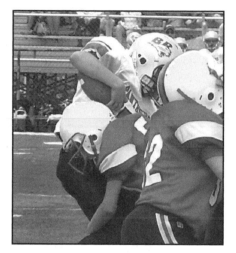

A: Wrap arms, drive shoulder, and drive legs.   B: Perfect postion: wrap, lift, drive.

Missed tackles are the main reason for offensive success. Kids often just try to grab the runner with their hands, and a hand tackle is very easy to break. Players need to understand that a tackle is the cornerstone of defense; it is glory time! It is time to explode and aggressively bring down the opponent. If a kid can't get excited at the moment of a tackle, he'll find no greater moment in football.

In a running situation, a side tackle, an ankle tackle, a tackle from behind, or a tackle falling in front of the runner is all that is available. The defender should try to get a shoulder into the runner, but he can't be choosy. He must muscle the runner down to the ground any way possible—but remember to focus, jolt, and wrap the arms when possible.

When rushing a passer, the defender should get his arms up high, waving them to obstruct vision or block the pass, then bring his arms crashing down upon the passer from above, wrapping his arms and hugging the passer to the ground.

TACKLING DRILLS

As with blocking, *form* is where to start, so get the defensive linemen into two (or three) rows, with each row having six players (two ends, two tackles, and two inside or nose guards) in their regular positions. Each line should be 10 feet from the next.

1. Form drill. This drill focuses on proper form. Since defensive linemen wait for their opponent to get into ready position before they drop into their three- or four- point stance, there is no need for a cadence. Just say "ready" and have them drop into their stance. Coaches roam about the lines pointing out stance corrections.

2. On the ball drill. Players line up in rows as stated above. The coach holds a ball on the line of scrimmage, calls out a quarterback cadence, and moves (hikes) the ball on a count of his choosing. Players charge forward on the hike. Coaches try to pull them offsides by staggering the cadence, or try to catch them asleep by hiking on no cadence at all. The idea is to promote attention upon the center's snap as the signal for when they must charge. Make sure their charge is vigorous.

3. Hold 'em drill. Have two evenly matched players line up at right angles to each other. One is a tackler and one is a ball carrier. To the side of the ball carrier away from the tackler, about 2 feet away, place an old mattress or gym mat. The tackler assumes proper tackling form, driving his shoulder low into the other player's thigh, arms wrapped around. Upon the whistle, the runner tries to break free from the tackle, and the tackler tries to lift, drive toward the mat, and bring him down. Let them switch positions. After a while, have the players each take a step back and run the same drill, with the tackler trying to assert good form and the runner going straight ahead but trying to avoid the tackle. Then separate them by two steps, but have them move at three-quarter speed. The mattress will catch most plays and help prevent bruises. Go over the *focus and wrap* section on page 66 and review each of the eight keys repeatedly.

4. Bull in the middle drill. This is a standard tackling form drill and should be done several times a week. Circle players in a ring with a 10-yard diameter. Choose a player to stand in the center to be the "bull." Throw the football to a player in the circle; he must try to get to the other side of the ring without being tackled by the bull. Then pick a new bull and throw to a new runner. Try to match kids of equal size. Have them run at three-quarter speed and focus entirely on form. As a coach, you must recognize good form and insist on it every time.

5. Pick a lane drill. Lay four tackling dummies parallel to each other about 6 feet apart. Have players line up on either side. One side gets the ball, and the first player in line runs with it into one of the lanes between the dummies. The first player on the other side tackles him. This is a three-quarter speed, full-contact drill (done in full pads), and it should be done once a week.

PASSING

By the turn of the twentieth century, football was perceived as a brutal and dangerous game. After a few tragedies, President Teddy Roosevelt called for reform, and soon the newly organized NCAA made changes, including legalizing the forward pass, which probably saved the game. Modern footballs are slimmer to facilitate the passing game.

Quarterbacks do much more than pass, and they need a unique combination of skills. However, to be a good passer, they should preferably be tall and have big hands, strong arms, good eyes, full field vision, courage, a knack for knowing when to release the ball, and, of course, throwing accuracy.

At the grade-school level, there are far fewer passes than at the high-school and college levels. The pros nowadays pass about half of the time, but each youth team runs maybe thirty-five to forty plays a game and throws the ball only a few times. Passing is the most complicated thing in football. A lot can go wrong, and interceptions occur often at youth levels. Turnovers are a heavy price to pay, and coaches worry about putting the ball in the air too much. I believe much of the problem comes from lack of proper form from the quarterback. A young quarterback is nervous, excited, and inexperienced, and the first thing to go under pressure is form. I doubt that youth coaches emphasize form enough. They seem to rely too much on the natural ability of their passers.

Learning the essentials of passing form creates a solid foundation for a young quarterback, and that greatly adds to his passing accuracy. If he practices these essentials, you will soon notice a difference in his poise, confidence, and success. The mechanics of passing are not difficult, but they must be practiced enough so that they become automatic. From such a foundation of strength and stability, your quarterback can perform at a higher level. I'll discuss pass patterns and routes in chapter five.

EIGHT KEYS OF PASSING

1. Think! A pass play begins as soon as the quarterback breaks from the huddle. He sizes up the defense. His gaze must be impassive, always starting from the same side of the field and slowly sweeping and scanning the secondary. What formation is the defense using? Can he spot a *blitz* (one or more defensive backs rushing across the line of scrimmage) coming? Is a defender out of position? Where are the seams, the spaces between defensemen? Where will there be a height mismatch? Has the wind changed and does it favor a long or short pass? How do things "feel"?

2. Take the snap comfortably. The quarterback's wrist and top hand should be firmly pressed against the center's crotch, firmly enough so that the center clearly knows exactly where they are. The passing hand is on top, other hand on the bottom. The insides of the wrists are touching with the fingers spread. (Some rotate the hand a bit so that the thumbs are up more—each quarterback should do what's comfortable.) The key is to take the snap securely and quickly. (See figure 4-14.)

3. Retreat quickly. A right-handed quarterback quickly turns to the right, pushes off with the left foot, and steps back with the right foot. On a running play up the middle (a dive), the quarterback must immediately present the ball for a handoff to the onrushing back. On a wider running play, he will have worked out the number of steps and his body angle over many practice runs. Sometimes he fakes a handoff to slow down the defensive charge. On a pass, some quarterbacks simply backpedal to their *pocket* area, a position 3 to 6 yards back where the offensive line will create a three-quarter ring of protection around him. Although backpedaling provides a clearer view of the secondary, there is a chance of tripping. Moreover, it clearly signals to the secondary that a pass play is forming, bringing them into pass coverage defense. Whatever method is used, the idea is to move back very quickly so there is time to track the downfield action. The snap, the footwork, the pivot, the quick drop-back, and the number of steps taken should be practiced repeatedly. The passer's hands should be kept high at the end of the retreat.

Quick-outs (passes to the flat) or quick slant passes may require only one to three steps. Most other passes require five steps, always starting and ending with the right

4-14. **QUARTERBACK SNAP POSITION**

The quarterback's form here is excellent: low, poised, and balanced.

foot (the back foot) if the quarterback is right-handed. A quarterback must practice these steps and make them routine. Fumbles or missteps will occur often if the quarterback is not comfortable with his passing routine. It must all be automatic, so that in a game situation, the passer can focus on his primary receiver and on the reaction of the defensive secondary.

4. Step forward. Once the passer *drops* (takes the prescribed and practiced number of steps backward) he should stop, pause, and then take a step forward. The outside pass rusher will usually rush in at an angle, running toward the expected back point of the quarterbacks drop, so the final step forward into the pocket affords more protection. Of course, if there is a weakness in the offensive line up the middle, and pressure comes from there, adjustments must be made. The quarterback may need to *roll out* to the flat or *scramble* to buy more time. He must stay cool, not panic,, and focus downfield so he can throw the pass—not recklessly or in desperation, but under control. And remember, a sack is always better than an interception.

5. Grip the ball, hands up at the shoulder. In the normal retreat, the quarterback should hold the ball up, even with the shoulder by the side of his head, using a proper passing grip in the throwing hand and protecting the ball with the other hand. The left or free hand should be kept on the ball, protecting it until ready to release it. This is a good habit; developing it early will definitely save a fumble. The ball should be gripped snugly, not squeezed, with the fingers spread wide and touching the ball along their entire length. The hand grips the ball in back of its center, with the pinky near the middle of the ball. The laces are under the last joints of the fingers. Some space should exist between the side of the palm and the ball. Again, comfort is desirable. A wide fingerspread is the best, but, of course, large hands are needed for that. Simple exercises manually stretching the fingers backward and sideways can improve the grip.

6. Survey, stand erect, hold the ball high, and step to the receiver. The quarterback's first job is to decide who gets the ball. Usually, it's already planned by the play pattern called in the huddle. The pattern will send two or three receivers into the defensive secondary, and it is designed so that the primary receiver winds up with only individual coverage, one-on-one. Sometimes even the timing of the throw is predetermined, so the passer knows about when the receiver will break to one side or speed up and go deep. The idea is to reach the receiver with the ball just after he breaks to one side, since that is when the defender is farthest from him, particularly if the receiver has faked convincingly to the other side. (See figure 4-15 A, B on page 72.)

4-15. QUARTERBACK PASSING POSTURE

A: Retreat with the ball high, protect it with the free hand, and look at developing pass patterns. Grip the laces under tip joint of fingers.

B. Ball is high, thrown from behind the ear.

Passers usually try to hit a receiver as he moves from one defensive zone to another, since he is most "open" when he is in the seam between defenders. However, the passer needs to be flexible enough to know how far the defender is from his primary receiver and to see if another defender is double-teaming his primary. Perhaps then he'll take a peek at his secondary receiver. The passer has only a second or two to do all of this. He must stand erect to get the fullest possible view, legs comfortable but not spread apart too much. His weight is on the back—usually the right—foot. The quarterback holds the ball high and then steps toward his target, toward where the receiver should be when the ball arrives. Taking too big a step causes a late release and an underthrown pass. The passer should take a comfortable, moderate step.

7. Snap the wrist. On a long pass, the nose of the ball should tilt up a bit so that it floats and settles safely into the receiver's hands. Of course, the farther the pass, the more the passer needs to lead the receiver. If there is to be a mistake on a long pass, it is better to err by overthrowing. The passer's arm must move straight since his weight is shifted to the front foot. His free arm is extended, preferably in the direction of the pass. The forward arm movement is very quick and snaps the wrist in a whipping motion, rolling the ball off the fingers, little finger first. The wrist snap causes the ball to spiral evenly; a nice spiral is easier to catch. The wrist brings the hand and fingers downward and inward as the ball rolls away. The spin need not, and should not, be too fast—just moderate.

A short pass needs an even harder wrist snap. It must be fired very hard since the ball must quickly thread its way through several outreaching defensive hands. It's usually better to underthrow a short pass if an error is to be made since there usually are more defenders deep. The nose of the ball should be level, or even down a hair, and the quarterback's arm should follow through fully.

8. Practice jump passes. Quarterbacks often have to throw passes while on the run, either in a designed roll-out play or during a scramble. Initially, the quarterback holds the ball to his side to hide it. Then, he raises and holds the ball high, faking the release if possible to slow a charging defender or perhaps get him to jump. If the secondary drops back, a run for yardage may be possible. Otherwise the quarterback should throw, remembering that less of a lead is needed if the receiver is moving in the same direction (to compensate for the passer's own momentum). If the passer must jump to get more torque on the pass (to allow his shoulders to open and turn toward the receiver) or to avoid a defender, the quarterback should release the ball with a quick wrist snap at the top of the jump. Taking the final step a bit forward, if possible, helps get some lost power on the ball. (See figure 4-16 on page 74.)

Passing drill. The best drill is to have two lines of receivers standing 10 feet on either side of the quarterback. Use two quarterbacks to alternate throws. Run the patterns you intend to use the most. Do a slant, 5 yards and cut across the middle, 10 yards and cut across the middle, and a down and out. See chapter five for discussion on passing routes.

The ideal pass is about 10 to 15 yards long, so practice these the most. Rest the arm on alternate days. Tell parents to remember that their son is throwing in practice, so their assistance is better saved for the off-season or during times when he has not been throwing too much. Do about twenty to thirty passes, going in and out. Throw some across the middle, some to the outside, and some that are quick, short passes.

4-16. JUMP PASS ON THE RUN

This is a tough pass, but often necessary, and it should be practiced

Don't wear out the passer's arm with too many long bombs. Save those for the end of practice when you are sure he has loosened up plenty.

Have quarterbacks (and all players, for that matter) practice with a wet ball. It will rain sometimes, and experience with a wet ball is very useful on such days. It's sometimes necessary to face the palm out more to maintain grip and contact on a wet ball for short passes. Let him attempt different approaches to find what works best. He should also pass off-balance in practice. I don't know why coaches don't practice it, but it does happen in games and that's what practice is for—to help execute better under game conditions. The hardest pass to make for a quarterback is when he is fading backward, it probably should not be thrown, but practice it anyway.

THE HANDOFF

The quarterback approaches a handoff to a running back with the ball securely held close in to his stomach with both hands. He focuses on the runner's midsection and extends his hands toward the ball carrier. (See figure 4-17 on page 75.) The hand closest to the runner drops away first, and the ball is directed into the area between the runner's arms (the arms are horizontal, with one across the upper abdomen and one across the lower abdomen). The running back's elbows need to be in a bit to not hit the quarterback. A good tip is to place the ball on the far hip of the runner to

4-17. **THE HANDOFF**

Hold the ball out, look at the runner's hands, and place the ball securely on the far hip.

ensure it gets planted firmly into the midsection. These handoffs must be practiced many times with the two players. The runner must be looking at the line to see the gap and the defense's movements, and so it's the quarterback's job to get the ball to the runner squarely. Drills can involve just the two players. Add the center after the quarterback and running back are in sync. Then drill with the entire backfield—quarterback and running backs—in formation, running actual play patterns. Do it quickly and get in a lot of repetitions.

It's also important to work on fake handoffs, since the defense will be looking for the ball. The idea is convince the defense that the quarterback has placed the ball into the running back's hands. The running back must also act as if he has the ball. The best technique is for the quarterback to hold the ball out to the runner and then quickly withdraw it. Another technique is for the quarterback to shield the ball on his hip and pretend to hand off the ball with his other hand, making a very quick movement toward the runner's midsection; the runner collapses his arms as if the ball was handed to him.

RECEIVING

Nothing gets a crowd going like the reception of a long, beautiful pass. Wide receivers are tall, agile athletes who are great leapers, have speed, and play with enormous courage. No one is hit as hard as a receiver coming down with his full weight into a helmet or shoulder of a tough defender.

You don't see many passes at the younger youth levels. Coaches know that the 50 percent completion rate in the pros is many times higher than the completion rate for nine- to thirteen-year-old kids. Interceptions are common at young ages. Again, this is an area where kids don't get a lot of work. In most states, as with many youth sports, there are limits to the amount of practice time kids get.

Here are some guidelines for receivers to follow.

1. Get off the line. I haven't seen many youth defenses that *check* or delay the offensive end or wide receiver at the line of scrimmage. If a defense does this, it is to delay the receiver so the quarterback has less time to pass. This move is more common in high school, perhaps because more passes are thrown at older ages. In any event, if someone tries to delay your player, he should use a quick, fake step to one side with arms out front, and perhaps a *shiver and shed* move. Sometimes, just a blast of speed around the defender is sufficient.

2. Run directly at the defender. This is a crucial first move. The natural impulse is to angle away from the defender, but that removes the ability to fake. The receiver should run hard right at the defender, as fast as possible, as if to run right through him. This takes away the defender's chance to anticipate the receiver's ultimate direction, and it should help to get the defender a bit off-balance.

3. Make the move just as the defender commits. Once the defender starts retreating, fully committed and backpedaling sufficiently, then the receiver should put on the next move. The receiver needs to concentrate on the defender's momentum. If he is backpedaling quickly, a fake may not be needed; the receiver can just cut quickly and sharply according to the pass pattern. However, a fake usually helps, so the receiver should take two or three steps to one direction and then cut sharply to the other. A head fake or a one-step fake is often not enough. The second or third step will change the defender's momentum and spring the receiver loose for the pass. This requires moving quickly, but under control, particularly in the final steps of the pattern. There is no need for full speed and the receiver should save a bit to allow for a reaction to the pass, which may be short or long.

4. Don't forget your quarterback. The quarterback is under tremendous pressure and may need to throw the pass early. The receiver must look to the quarterback as soon as the receiver breaks from his fake. The receiver must forget the defender for a moment, and make eye contact with the passer as quickly as possible—he needs some attention immediately. Too many times, receivers don't do this and passes fall close to them without them realizing it.

5. Focus, have soft hands, and wait for the ball. When the ball is in the air, quick decisions have to be made. The receiver adjusts his speed to meet the ball. Eyes must be on the ball. The receiver must not reach for it until it gets close, since that will tip off the defender as to its timing. Often, the defender will turn his back on the ball and watch the receiver's body language as his signal for when it's time to turn for the ball. So, again, the receiver must not reach early, and must try to remain calm. The arms and hands should be relaxed, with soft fingers ready to receive the ball; the hands are gently withdrawn upon contact with the ball to soften the impact.

6. Catch it high, use the hands, and curl and spread fingers. A pass should be caught as high in the air as possible. First, this reduces the chance for an interception. Second, it gets the receiver off the ground. The body is smooth as it glides through the air, but it is bumpy while running; getting off the feet helps for a smooth catch.

The receiver should catch with the hands and curl the fingers. The fingers should curl into the form of the ball. If they are straight, the ball tends to bounce off the palm. Too often, kids try to trap the ball with their arms. It's okay to use the chest and arms to trap the ball, especially in traffic, but the hands are always more effective.

Tell your players to try this: Focus on the front tip of the ball and try to catch it. It really helps to focus concentration and hand placement. Watching the ball all the way into the hands is critical. Tell him to watch the spin of the ball or try to see the laces spinning as he catches it. A receiver has a certain "oneness" with the ball. He should feel as though he has already caught it while it is still in the air. (See figure 4-18 on page 78.)

In a *deep pattern*, the receiver arches his back and raises his hands, palms back. On a *buttonhook* (see the glossary), he faces the ball, hands in a W shape. On a pass across the middle, the best place to catch the ball is just in front of the inside shoulder.

The receiver must catch and tuck the ball in before running. This may sound obvious, but kids often think about running before they secure the catch, or maybe they are bracing for an expected hit. The most important job for a receiver is to firmly catch and tuck the ball before doing anything else.

7. Change direction immediately. The defense tends to flow with the receiver's momentum and direction, so making an immediate change of direction after a reception is usually quite effective. The move is particularly recommended when the receiver does not know where the defensive coverage is around him. It helps to break away for a few more yards, or perhaps spring a long run. A spin move also helps at this point. However, the receiver must always remember that the most important thing is to have the ball tucked in securely.

8. Recover and tackle if intercepted. If the pass is intercepted, chances are the intended receiver has the best first shot at the tackle. He should recover immediately, not get mad at himself, and not turn into a spectator. Now his job is to get the opponent and bring him down.

RECEIVING DRILLS

As with passing, the best receiving drill is just doing it. If your receiver is young, you may wish to throw while down on one knee to simulate the height of the normal ball release of his quarterback. If there are a few kids around, set them up in a secondary to simulate defensive coverage and keep throwing passes to your intended receiver. Have your checklist (found on page 169) handy and keep calling out helpful hints. It's good for your receiver to practice catching passes with one hand. Throw to one side, then to the other. It helps to train the hands to react properly.

4-18. **RECEIVING**

The hands should be up and the eyes on the ball.

RUNNING

At the grade-school level, football is a running game. The great majority of plays involve running the ball, and most yardage seems to be gained on wide running sweeps. Often, the team with a real speedster breaks open big plays around the end of the line to score. Of course, plays are also run up the middle, but blocking techniques are usually not very well developed yet, so defensive linemen and linebackers pretty much control the middle.

Most people seem to feel that the glory of football is found at the running back position. I guess over the years the Jim Browns and the Walter Paytons of the game have gotten the most exposure. Anyone who has played football has great respect for all positions; however, the running backs put the numbers up on the scoreboard. They get hit very hard and earn every bit of their attention. My son played fullback his first year, and while he didn't have great speed, he used to buck the line with a full and reckless abandon, dropping his shoulder and often giving a linebacker a shot of his own.

TOP SIX RUNNING FUNDAMENTALS

1. Get into the stance. The runner needs a stance from which he can move in any direction with ease and quickness. As with the linemen, runners start from a ready position—feet spread apart, hands on the knees, and eyes straight ahead. Then they drop into a set position. Some coaches prefer them to stay up in ready position since this allows for a better read of the developing hole they must run through, but it sacrifices quickness.

Since most running plays, except for dives straight up the middle, require lateral movement, a runner must be able to move laterally very quickly. A spread and balanced foot position allows for a push to either side, so in the set position a runner's legs are fairly wide apart. One foot, usually the inside foot, is set back, but only a few inches behind the front. This helps balance. The hand on the same side as the back foot is straight down, but not much weight is on it. It is mainly for balance. The head is up and the back is straight like a lineman's. The body is tense, coiled, and ready to spring. The toes are straight ahead, or even pointed outward since the push comes from the inside front or balls of the feet.

It is essential to get into exactly the same stance every play. The defense is looking intently for a clue as to where the play will go. The running backs must not help them out by leaning or looking to where the play will go. Head, shoulders, and eyes are forward and impassive.

2. Pivot and snap. Running backs must fully pivot toward their intended direction before they ever take a step. They snap the head and shoulders in that direction, shifting weight by pushing off the ball of the foot opposite to that direction. Only *after* the pivot do they take the first, large step, with the foot closest to the intended direction. Stepping first just wastes time. It is much quicker to pivot first and then step out directly. This technique must be practiced until it is automatic. The head and shoulder snap adds to the overall quickness of the move. The idea is to take off low, stay low, and then build up speed with strong, churning arm movement.

As I watch pre-high-school games, I am struck by how long it takes for the backfield action to develop. The problem is often that the running back gets to the hole too late. A blocker gives a jolt, as described earlier, and attempts to sustain the block, but the defender uses his hands freely to shed him. Therefore, the running back must get there before the defender fully recovers. A split second makes all the difference, especially at young ages when sustained blocking is the exception and not the rule. The 4 or 5 yards between the running back and the line of scrimmage are critical. Getting to the hole quickly is more important than what happens later. In fact, the first move—the pivot and snap—is the most important of all.

3. Look at the hole; receive the handoff securely. A running back should not worry about the quarterback. The quarterback's job is to get the ball to the runner safely. The runner must look at the gap in the defense that he will run through. He scrutinizes the area to see what is developing and to see whether a key block will be successful.

As noted on page 74, the quarterback should present the ball firmly to the runner, usually with one hand on the outside and underside of the ball, well into the runner's midsection, just above the belt. The quarterback should focus squarely on the runner's belt. When a play is into the middle of the line, the runner receives the ball with his far arm relaxed down in front of the opposite hip, palm toward the ball, and the elbow and forearm nearest the quarterback raised chest high, ready to help cover and secure the ball. He then curls both hands around the opposite tips of the ball, covering the tips—not just circling them. On a wide play, the runner may receive the ball in his midsection, or he may take it with his hands, depending on the speed and motion needed.

4. Carry the ball securely. Most fumbles do not occur because of a powerful defensive jolt, but because the ball was not carried securely. In one game, my son's team lost the ball on the first play of their first two possessions because the same running back carried the ball through the line like it was a flag, waving it around wildly.

The proper carrying technique is to carry the ball high, jamming the point of the ball into the pocket between the upper arm and ribs, just below the armpit. The forearm is stretched along the side of the ball, slightly to the underside. The hand is curled around the front tip, fingers spread to the inside. The technique is designed to protect the ball, and every protection is needed. The other arm can swing free to gain speed or agility, but in close traffic or upon a tackle, the other arm is placed across the ball to add protection. Tacklers not only hit hard, but they are instructed to tear or slash the ball free, especially the second tackler on the scene. (See figure 4-19.)

The ball is carried in the right arm when running right and in the left arm when running left. When running in the open field, the runner may switch hands to get the ball away from the nearest approaching tackler, but only if he is absolutely sure there is time. He must make sure the new hand has the ball before sliding it across the midsection for the switch.

5. Give a second effort. Once the ball is secured and the runner is in motion, it's time to get yardage. The single focus of the running back must be to get as much yardage as possible. He doesn't worry about the tackler; he looks mainly for holes in the defense. When a tackler appears, the ball carrier continues to run hard—to get that precious yardage. A good running back avoids the tackler's shoulder, runs right through his

4-19. **SECURE THE BALL**

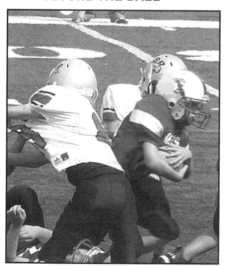

Secure the ball snugly up in the armpit, and cover it with the free hand when in traffic.

arms, twists, turns, and keeps his legs underneath his body with short, driving steps. He falls forward or lunges for the extra few inches. One of the truly beautiful phrases in football is *second effort*. Second effort refers to those extra few yards a running back fights for even after the defense has made contact with him. This determination to fight through contact is what makes a great running back.

6. Use the stiff-arm and other maneuvers. I don't see the stiff-arm, or *straight-arm*, used as much as it should be used, yet it is a most useful weapon against the tackle. The idea is to reach out just as the tackler lunges and place the palm out onto his shoulder or helmet. Then the ball carrier points his shoulder at the tackler and firmly straightens and locks the arm. The runner must not give the arm too early or the tackler will avoid (or grab) it. As soon as his arm makes contact, the runner should leap a bit. This substantially reduces the tackler's jolt and can catapult the runner a few yards. A stiff-arm can also be effective to push the tackler down or away, particularly if he is off-balance.

Another move is the *step-out*, in which the runner jabs a sharp step toward the tackler to make him tense up, then pushes off laterally away from him, perhaps with a straight-arm. The runner can also pivot away from a jab step by planting his other foot and then swinging the foot that initiated the jab step in a full 360-degree turn away from the defender's momentum.

The *crossover* is a third avoidance measure in which the leg nearest the tackler is lifted high and away as the body also leans away. This is usually effective on a sweep or wide play before the defender gets too close.

Even though maneuvers such as the straight-arm, step-out, and crossover can be useful, more often the runner bucks the line on a dive or off-tackle run, that is, he runs laterally from a plugged-up hole along the line of scrimmage, behind his blockers, keeping the body low and looking for another hole or just one more inch.

SPECIALTIES

Special teams are used for kicking—primarily for kickoffs, field goals, points after touchdowns, and punts. As you can see, these teams are on the field mainly when possession is being formally transferred to the opponent (kickoff and punt) or when attempting to score by place-kicking (a field goal or a point after touchdown). The action is often spread over the entire field with players running at full speed. There are some unique and quite important skills involved, particularly kicking skills, and players

should seriously consider developing them. For nine to thirteen year olds, the kicks in the kickoff normally range from 20 to 35 yards, increasing about 4 to 5 yards each year. More often than not, the ball is miskicked and travels close to the ground, bouncing after 15 yards. Have your players try punting and place-kicking, particularly if any of them have played soccer. Good kickers are very rare and are valuable to grade-school teams. With a bit of practice, it is incredible how quickly a youngster can improve. Most kids just never try to kick. Other specialties such as catching punts and kickoffs and hiking the snaps for kickers are also important.

THE SNAP

In the professional leagues, the punter lines up 12 to 15 yards behind the line of scrimmage. At youth levels, it is 7 to 12 yards, depending on the age, and that's still quite a long hike for a young center. The field goal or point after touchdown snap is a few yards shorter; place kicks are still quite rare at the youth level. The center should practice the snap regularly, preferably with the team's actual punter or place-kick holder. The snap is similar to an upside-down pass: the harder and faster, the better. A fast snap can save a precious split second and avoid a blocked punt. A good practice drill for the snapper is to throw a few 10-yard forward passes with the second hand on and guiding the ball, then just bend over and do it from between the legs.

The center should get into a normal stance, with the back foot a bit farther back if that is more comfortable. He then raises the front point of the ball and places the right hand up near the front of the ball, similar to a passer's grip. His left hand is on the side of the ball to help guide it, particularly if his hands are small. The left hand leaves the ball first. Weight is moderately forward upon the ball, as is normal for snaps. Driving the ball back in a quick, snapping motion, the center aims for the area between the punter's knee and waist, or directly to the hands of the place-kick holder. He should give the ball as little arc as possible and make the snap hard. Finally, he must make sure that the snap is completed before worrying about blocking the nose guard; the snap is more important than the guard. Blocked punts are always a major disaster. Bracing and stepping forward with the snap for balance helps avoid bad snaps.

PUNTING

Punting is often avoided at the very young ages unless long yardage is needed for a first down or the team is backed up very near to their own goal line. The potential for punting disasters is quite high. A bad snap, poor blocking, or a slow punter all

83

combine to discourage coaches from trying it, particularly when the successful kick often gains only 10 to 15 yards. Coaches figure the heck with it. They take their chances with a sweep around the end and hope to get lucky.

But if you are going to attempt a punt, here are the keys. Before the ball is snapped, the punter surveys the plant area in front of him to ensure that there is good footing. He then looks only at the ball. His feet are parallel. His weight is on the left foot if he is a righty. The arms are extended outward, palms down and inward, thumbs up, fingers spread and curled a bit. He stands erect, hands soft, body relaxed.

As the ball is snapped, he concentrates and lets the ball come all the way to his hands. The hands should withdraw slightly to soften contact. He rotates the ball to get the laces up and places the right hand back a bit, cradling the ball. He takes a short step with the kicking foot and a second longer and quicker step with the other foot, planting it firmly and securely. Extending and serving the ball over the kicking leg with the front of the ball pointed downward a little and turned slightly to the inside, the punter places the ball on his foot with the right hand. He must not drop it too far; the less distance it travels between the hand and the foot, the better.

The kick will spiral if the ball is kicked with the outside of the instep, with the right side of the shoelaces contacting the underbelly of the ball. It will travel end over end if kicked on the instep squarely along the bottom seam of the ball. The knee is at first relaxed. As it comes forward, it whips the rigidly locked ankle forward in a hard snapping motion to give power and distance to the punt. (See figure 4-20 on page 85.) The foot comes forward in a smooth pendulum motion, not sideways, and snaps through to shoulder height, at least, pulling the body forward in a hopping motion. The left arm may raise up and swing across the chest to help balance and torque.

The punter only has a couple of seconds to do all of this. He must be quick, balanced, and under control. A good practice drill is to have the punter kick softly, about 5 to 10 yards to a teammate (or to a parent), watching his form and point of contact with the ball and trying to lay the ball on the instep with as little extra distance as possible. Have him tap it to you, and he should learn enough control so you don't have to move to catch it at all. Then, have him overcompensate the other way, booming kicks for maximum power and distance. He should try to get the kick away in about two seconds from the snap.

When punting from the defensive half of the field, its important to ensure the ball does not reach the end zone. If it does, the opponent is awarded a touchback

4-20. PUNTING FORM

Punts are often avoided at youth levels because kickers don't kick very far. Practicing punts can make a player a rare and valuable asset.

and their offense will begin play at their 20-yard line. So the punter kicks the ball toward the sideline trying to kick it so it goes out of bounds between to goal line and the twenty yard line. The opponent must begin from wherever it goes out of bounds, so a great punt will go out of bounds inside the 5-yard line. Practice these angled punts.

CATCHING PUNTS

When the other team is punting to your team, have your receiver stand about 5 yards deeper than the punter can kick so he is moving forward as he receives the ball. This could add at least 5 yards to the return. The receiver should have his arms raised forward and upward a bit. Palms should be up, fingers spread, and hands fairly close together. The ball should always be caught with the hands and then brought into the midsection quickly for protection. The body and hands should withdraw, even squat a bit, to soften impact. Once he catches the ball, the receiver executes the return play called by the coach, looking for open space and avoiding tacklers with fakes and feints. (See figure 4-21 on page 86.)

PLACE KICKING

Soccer-style kicking has pretty much taken over football. It gives just as much power and much more accuracy than the toe kicking of olden days. If a player has a good strong foot, try him at place kicking.

4-21. **RECEIVING PUNTS**

Receive the ball with the hands and quickly bring it into the body.

KICKING FIELD GOALS

The kicker lines up behind and to one side of the holder at a distance that allows for the number of steps he personally needs to execute a proper kick (usually two or three) in a quarter-circle motion that ends with his planting (the non-kicking) foot astride the ball. He first steps off the needed distance and stands with legs even, leaning forward a bit on the front foot. The holder kneels on his left knee near where he will place the ball, right leg extended forward, arms reaching toward the ball. He receives the snap, lowers the ball to the spot, turns the laces facing forward (out of the way of the foot), and places the end of his right hand exactly on the tip, removing his left hand. He looks only at the ball. It should be nearly straight up, or tilted a tiny bit backward, depending on the kicker's preference. The kicker takes two or three steps and firmly plants the free foot pointing straight at the target, toes even with the back of the ball and several inches to the side, depending on the kicker's comfort and style. He snaps the kicking foot into the lower half of the ball. (See figure 4-22 A, B on page 87.)

KICKOFFS

The kickoff is just a long place kick, except that the kicker takes numerous steps, covering at least 5 yards, and the ball is kicked off a tee. Otherwise, the techniques are the same. (See figure 4-22 C.) Kids can kickoff at a range of 20 to 40 yards. If a kid can consistently deliver 30 or more yards by age ten, he should try out for this position.

4-22. **PLACEKICKING**

A: Hold the ball with the index finger of right hand. Make sure the ball is straight with the laces away from kicker.

B: Plant foot firmly; keep eyes on the ball; snap foot forward.

C: Kickoff is a long place kick and requires a longer step and stronger snap of the foot.

05 OFFENSE: CONCEPTS AND FORMATIONS AND THE COACH'S PLAYBOOK

Here, it starts to get a bit complicated. And if it's complex to you, think about how a kid may struggle to grasp football strategy. One major difference between football and other sports is that the action on the field is much more controlled. Each offensive play is fully and precisely diagrammed and repeatedly practiced. Boys must line up on the practice field and run through play patterns endlessly. They are expected to run plays smoothly. The handoff of the ball to the running back and his movement through a hole in the line of scrimmage must be properly timed. Blocking assignments are carefully planned out, and passing routes are measured to the step.

Other sports have play patterns, but none are as precisely worked out as in football. Basketball has specific offensive patterns, but there is much more flexibility. Soccer, at the other extreme, flows according to opportunities of the moment. In football, the plays are preprogrammed. However, players must also react to the situation at hand, since the defense has no intention of cooperating.

This chapter will discuss general concepts of offense. (Chapter six will do the same for defense.) These general principles of motion and strength are what coaches and players should understand. I will review and recommend specific player formations, explain how and why they differ, and what the line-ups offer to the overall strategy. I will also review the most common play patterns used in youth football. Finally, I will present a playbook that diagrams specific plays from select offensive formations against various defenses.

You can help a player greatly if you discuss the underlying concepts of offensive and defensive play with him. It will broaden his perception of what's going on around him. Once a player understands why things are done a certain way, he can perform more intelligently.

TOP TEN OFFENSIVE CONCEPTS

1. Know your plays. You often see players looking around wondering what to do. They have either forgotten the play or don't know how to block against an unexpected defensive formation. Good execution of a blocking and running pattern against a given defense is more rare than you would think. It takes only one weak link to mess up a play. More often than a bad block, you will see no block at all. Kids must know their assignments against various defenses, and the team should practice them repeatedly. Coaches in youth football underestimate this need more than any other. Remember, these are kids and even simple play patterns can be confusing.

Understanding the play, the entire play, is probably the most underrated concept in football. Some coaches think linemen will just block the player nearest to them and all will be well. But to succeed as a team, each player must know each play completely. They should be aware of what they have to do, what everyone else has to do, and how to do it against the several defenses they may face. They should walk through each play against dummy defenses and run it live against different defenses. Knowing the play means more than knowing what to do as an individual; it means knowing what the team is trying to do. This is the most important offensive concept, period. Know what to do by knowing what *everyone* is doing.

2. Control possession of the ball. The bread-and-butter play of football is the *power running play*—the dive or blast up the middle or the off-tackle play aimed at the hole between the tackle and end. It's tough for kids because of poor blocking, but it's what wins games at every level. If a team can successfully and consistently run the ball and slowly chew up yardage, gaining 3 to 5 yards per play, they will use up a lot of time. This means that the other team will have the ball for a lesser portion of the game. It's hard to score if you don't have the ball. At youth levels, a good drive down the field, let's say 70 yards, takes about fifteen plays and can consume an entire quarter of the game. More importantly, sustained offensive drives lead to good field position, and this will increase the chance that a big play will score. As in any sport, luck is a large part of football, and teams often break a big play for a score. But if you reduce the amount of time that the other team has possession of the ball, you will reduce the time they have to make such a play.

Football is more of a running game at the Pop Warner level than it is in high school. As mentioned earlier, the big running plays are often wide sweeps by a really fast kid who outruns everyone and breaks away for a score. However, the more conservative run up the middle is the cornerstone of good offense. On first down, try to run a slant or blast between the tackle and the end to get 5 yards. Then you'll have two more shots at the next 5 yards. If your team can do this consistently, they will be very successful.

3. Open a hole; penetrate the defensive line. If you want to advance the football, you need to open a hole in the defensive wall so the runner can get by. Defense usually outnumbers offense since the quarterback does little blocking and thus ten blockers face eleven tacklers. Plus, defenders try to hit the gaps that the running backs are trying to go through. The objective of every running play is to get the ball carrier through the first line of defense. If you do, you will gain at least a few yards and perhaps the runner can put a move on the linebacker to get more yardage.

Sure, a really strong kid can block a defensive lineman and just shove him out of the way, creating a hole. However, younger kids are usually of similar strength, and a straight driving block often results in a stalemate. You have to get smart. The keys to opening a hole are a) *slant blocking*, that is, blocking from an angle; b) double-teaming a player; or c) trapping a key defensive lineman. (See figure 5-1.)

If you can get blockers into a position where they are attacking target defenders from an angle, their jobs will be much easier. It's tough to block big, strong, defensive tackles head-on. They are usually the strongest players on the team. If you approach them from the side, you can avoid their strength. Plays are usually designed to provide as much slant blocking as possible.

4. Lead the play through the hole (power football). Numbers win in youth ball, so you should run plays that get a lot of blockers in front of the ball. Often, a hole will open on the line, but a linebacker or defensive secondary player will quickly plug it.

5-1. SLANT BLOCKING

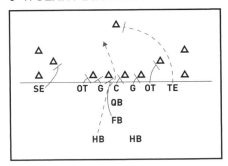

The most effective block for youths is the slant, hitting an opponent from the side angle. Here, the center and right guard slant block to their right while the left guard and left tackle double-team their lineman.

5-2. LEAD THROUGH THE HOLE

Here the guard (#68) pulls to lead the play around the end.

Usually, someone on the offensive line is assigned to block the linebacker, but it is a very tough block to make. The offensive response is to have someone lead the play through the hole. You send a player into the hole ahead of the ball carrier to block the first defender who gets to the hole. You usually send a blocking back (such as the fullback) or pull a guard to do this job. (See figure 5-2.)

If all of these efforts fail and the hole is not opened, or if it closes very quickly, then the ball carrier is on his own. He can try to bull his way through for a yard or two, or change direction and try his luck elsewhere, looking for a gap in the defense.

5. Run short, pass long. If it is third down and you have 2 yards to go for a first down, odds are that you can pick up the 2 yards with a power play diving up the middle with your strongest running back, usually the fullback. However, if it's third down and nine, or, you've received a penalty and it's second down and nineteen, then you have a long way to go. Since running plays usually average only a few yards each, in long-yardage situations, the odds are better to throw the ball. A pass play can get 10 to 15 yards—even more if the receiver can avoid the first tackler. Thus, run for short yardage, pass for long yardage. Your offensive strategy must take into consideration the down and how many yards you have to go.

6. Screen or draw an aggressive defense. I noted earlier that a defender's primary job is to control his area. There can be a passive aspect that just says, "Don't let anybody get by." However, sometimes the defense is very aggressive, maybe a bit stronger than other teams you've faced. They seem to easily penetrate your offensive line and get into the offensive backfield. This is disastrous. A good coach will spot it happening and use the defense's momentum to help his team.

In such a circumstance, a *screen play* should be tried. The blockers give the rushing defenders a jolt to slow them up, then let them go by. The quarterback drops back and lofts a soft, short pass over the onrushing defense to a receiver who now has the blockers in front of him.

Trap blocks are also useful against onrushing defenders in a *draw play*. Here, the running back hesitates a second to give a pulling lineman time to get to his blocker. Then the quarterback hands off the ball, and just as the tackler thinks he will make a big tackle in the backfield, he is creamed by that pulling lineman from the side and taken out of the play. (See figure 5-3.)

7. Misdirect and counter. Another useful play concept is to sweep the backs in one direction to get the defense moving that way, then hand off to a running back who counters against the flow. The blockers then have it easier since the motion pulls the defense away from the actual play. However, if the defense is focused on the linemen and not the backs, it does not work as well.

8. Sweep your speedster. A coach must go with the hand he is dealt. If he has an extremely fast running back, he can run him wide around the whole pack. To take advantage of his speed, first soften up the defense with a dive play, and then, on the next play, have your speedster simply run around it.

A *pitchout* is a good way to give your back a head start on an end sweep. (See figure 5-4.) In a pitchout, the speedster lines up off-tackle and darts outside immediately upon the snap. The quarterback quickly *laterals* (passes the ball sideways or backwards) or pitches the ball underhand to the speedster, who then sprints to the sideline to turn the corner for some yardage. On such a play, he is on his own. No blockers can get out

5-3. **TRAP BLOCK ON DRAW PLAY**

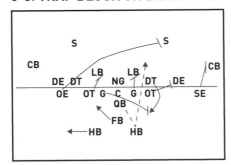

The defensive tackle comes across, toward the right halfback and is trapped by the left guard.

5-4. **SWEEP THE SPEEDSTER**

Here, the quickest player runs to the outside and beats the defense downfield. This is most effective play in youth football; speed wins games.

fast enough to help. It's just speed against speed. If a team is blessed enough to have someone with such speed, the sweep play is a great tool.

9. Spread out the defense. When a team runs plays up the middle a lot, the defense tends to bunch up in the middle. The offensive coach can force the defense to open up by splitting out a few wide receivers along the line of scrimmage, or by running a sweep or some pass plays to spread out the linebackers and secondary. If they don't spread out, then keep the action wide. *Razzle-dazzle* is a fancy term—it's an over-glorified collection of trick plays that usually means a team can't overpower the defense and has to resort to complicated plays like reverses or flea-flickers. But it does tend to open up the defense. A *reverse* is a play in which the quarterback hands off to a running back going wide, who in turn hands off to another player going the opposite way. The idea is to get the defense going in one direction and then have the speedster suddenly switch to going the other way to go around the whole pack. A *flea-flicker* is a play in which the quarterback hands off to a running back who takes a few steps forward and then turns and flicks the ball back to the quarterback, who then throws a long pass. The idea is to get the defensive backs to think it's a running play; they come forward, and the receiver scampers past them for the long pass. There are also *option plays* explained on pages 102–103.

Razzle-dazzle can break open a big play, but it can also lead to a big loss if the defense is not outsmarted. The plays take a long time to execute, and a lot can go wrong. You don't see too much of this action in youth football.

10. Take it to the airways. As mentioned earlier, passes are not often thrown at the youth level. Kids don't catch very well, the passes are not accurate, and pass blocking is usually poor (for reasons I can't understand, since pass blocking is the easiest thing in football). A passing game is usually risky, with a high potential for interceptions. The toughest part about youth passing seems to be the timing. Quarterbacks tend to hold the ball too long. They don't hit the receiver when he is in the *seam* (an open area between defenders). I often see a receiver wide open across the middle, but the quarterback doesn't pass the ball to him until the receiver's reached deep coverage and is no longer free. In any event, if a team is up against a tough defense and cannot run the ball, they have to go to the air and hope to get lucky.

I believe the most effective passes at the youth level are passes to the tight end in the flat, crossing behind a wide receiver who slants in. (See figure 5-5 on page 94.) For some reason, this area is often open. A deep bomb is a dangerous play, and passes

05

across the middle usually find a lot of congestion. But a screen—a short pass to the flat—is a good tool, particularly if the quarterback has speed and can roll out toward the sidelines. If the pass is across the middle, I recommend a very quick, short throw. The quarterback doesn't drop back, and he tosses the ball over the middle to a big tight end who finds some open space. (See figure 5-6.) It must be very quick. The backs head to each side of the center to stop a blitz and/or freeze the linebacker.

OFFENSIVE FORMATIONS

At college and pro levels, and even at high-school levels, a smart coach uses several different offensive formations in each game to exploit individual weaknesses in the opponent's defense or to maximize the abilities of his own talent. The differences in offensive formations are in how the running backs and receivers are positioned. Where these players are positioned will affect how spread out the defense is, how close the ball carrier is to his target hole, and how best to confuse the defense. Formations can be grouped into general categories such as the *wing offense*, which includes the single-wing, wing-T, and double-wing formations. These formations move one or two running backs to positions just behind and outside of a tight end or into a *wing back position.*

Some formations favor the running play; others favor the pass. Rules require that the offense have at least seven players on the line of scrimmage, so the five interior linemen almost always line up the same way and vary only in how close they are to each

5-5. **PASS TO THE FLAT**

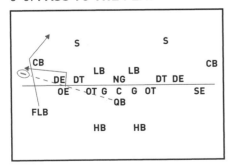

The wide receiver, here a flankerback, takes the cornerback deep, and so the tight end should be free in the flat.

5-6. **QUICK SLANT PASS**

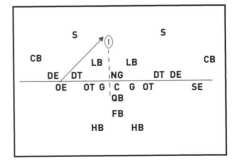

The tight end slants directly across the middle with a very quick dash and grabs a pass. The quarterback doesn't even drop back, but just quickly fires the pass.

other. However, the placement of the backs and receivers can vary greatly. In the following sections, I'll review the evolution of formations, identify the most popular youth football formations, and recommend specific approaches for various age groups.

EVOLUTION OF FORMATIONS

Figure 5-7 shows two formations, the single-wing and the T, that were very popular in the early days of football but are not used much anymore. Both of these formations are classic running or power formations and were used exclusively in the days before passing was allowed.

The single-wing formation is even older than the T. It overloads the backs to one side and snaps the ball directly to a running back set 4 to 5 yards behind the center. The single-wing allows the offense to shift its strength to one side, adding greatly to their ability to run power plays to that side. Since this play was used prior to the rule requiring the offense to be set for a full second before the snap, the offense had a big advantage. This formation is complex in its blocking assignments and is tough for youth teams to learn. Nowadays its value is in passing, since it includes a shotgun-type snap, where the ball is hiked to the quarterback, who stands about 6 to 9 feet (in youth ball) behind the center. But, as we know, youth football is not about passing. Moreover, the long snap is tricky to master and creates problems of its own.

In response, the T-formation was introduced to provide the running game with more blocking and flexibility. The T is a tough, power-running formation. It's good for youth football; however, with all three running backs in the backfield, it bunches up the defense. Most teams want an offensive play to spread things out a bit more. In the

5-7. EARLY FOOTBALL FORMATIONS

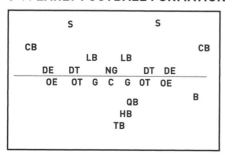

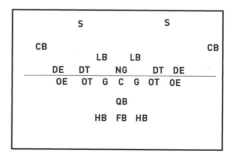

A: The Single-Wing. In the single-wing, the ball is hiked directly to a tailback or a halfback. The power is shifted entirely to one wing.

B: The T. In the T-formation, all backs are able to hit any hole or block for any other back. It's a pure and powerful running formation.

deceptive T-formation, three running backs can strike any place on the line and can also block for each other. The ends stay in tight to block.

The forward pass is what revolutionized offensive formations. Coaches quickly realized they needed to spread out their receivers to create one-on-one opportunities against the defense. First came the *open formation*. It split one of the ends out wide along the line of scrimmage on one side and placed a flankerback out wide on the other side. This formation not only increased the chance for these two wide receivers to face one-on-one coverage, it also spread out the defense to the benefit of the running game. The open formation posed a balanced threat for both the run and the pass. (See figure 5-8 on page 97.)

Other formations were developed over the years. The *twin set formation* is similar to the open formation except that it places both wide receivers on the same side, allowing them to work crossing patterns off each other. The *veer formation* is also used. It's similar to a twin set formation except the running backs line up wider, almost behind the tackles, to open things up more and allow plays like the triple option.

Finally, the ultimate passing formation, the *single back* or *lone set back*, arrived on the scene, allowing for three wide receivers. Of course, the lone running back has no other back to block for him, but some of the game's great running backs proved they could still gain yardage, especially since the defense was so spread out trying to cover passes.

In the past ten years, we've seen the pros use formations with no one in the backfield, the ultimate in passing formations. The Dallas Cowboys popularized the *shotgun formation*. Here, the quarterback takes the snap from 4 to 5 yards (in the pros) behind the center. This formation helps the quarterback to make a successful pass, since he can start looking at the defensive coverage immediately, without having to backpedal first. One or two backs are usually kept back to block in this formation.

CONTEMPORARY YOUTH FOOTBALL FORMATIONS

In a kid's first few years of football, he will not see many purely passing formations. However, several good running formations are used. I'll review what I think are the best three.

Modern coaches still prefer to use split ends to take a cornerback away from the action and open up the defense. Coaches have also learned that it's good to give the blocking back, usually the fullback, an extra step to get more quickly to his target. Thus, instead of the T-formation, you see the *wishbone formation* at younger ages. Youth football is a running game, and the wishbone is very effective at the run. It provides much of the running power of the old T-formation, and by setting the fullback closer to the hole, it adds speed to a dive. It also gives him more time as a blocking back to get to the linebacker. It utilizes a split end to open the defense up.

The *I-formation* is another popular formation, and your defense will surely see a lot of it; you should learn it even if you don't use it. You should run it against your first defense at practices. It is like the open formation in that it uses a split end on the

5-8. COMBINED PASSING AND RUNNING FORMATIONS

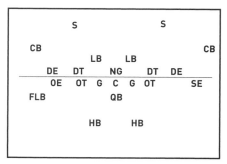

A: The Open Set. In the open formation, the defense is opened up for a balanced run or pass attack. Two backs are positioned to run or pass block, and two receivers—a flanker, and a split end—are wide for a pass.

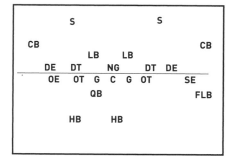

B: The Twin Set. The twin set is just like the open formation except that both wide receivers are on one side. This allows them to make moves off each other, such as crossing patterns.

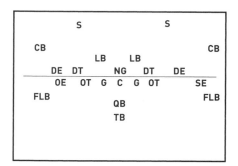

C: The Lone Set Back. This is one of the purest of passing formations and is used regularly in the pros. There is one single set back and three wide receivers. A variation lines up all three receivers on one side in an I-formation, thus overloading the protection on that side.

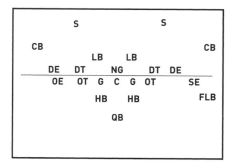

D: The Shotgun. The center performs a long snap back to the quarterback, who is positioned to immediately focus on the pass pattern.

weak side and a flanker on the strong side; however, the running backs, a fullback and a tailback, are in a straight line behind the quarterback. Like the T-formation, it's good for power plays up the middle, but it also spreads out the defense by setting out a flankerback. It's particularly effective with a very good running back, since it focuses on one primary running back. (See figure 5-9.) A variation is the *slot-I*, in which the flanker lines up on the strong side in the slot between the split end and the tackle. The *power-I* is an effective power variation where the flanker lines up next to the fullback. Occasionally a team lines up in an unbalanced line or *offset-I*, with the *I* more to one side, which serves to confuse the defense. If the defense does not shift, the offense has more players on that side and thus more power to that side of the center.

Finally, there is the *double-wing* formation; it's not prevalent, but it is gaining popularity with coaches. This formation positions both backs in the wing position

5-9. **MODERN YOUTH FOOTBALL FORMATIONS**

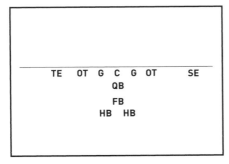

A; The Wishbone. This is a running formation much like the old T-formation except that the fullback is pulled up closer to make dive plays quicker and also to block quicker.

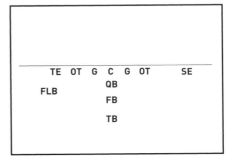

B: The I. The I-formation is much like the open formation as it allows for a balanced passing and running game. The I-shape lineup helps to conceal the play and gives more power up the middle.

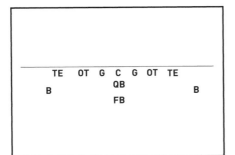

C: The Double-Wing. This is an emerging youth formation. Since wingbacks are so spread out, play patterns can include misdirection yet still bring power to bear at the point of contact.

just outside each end. The quarterback is on the center with a lone fullback behind him. The original double-wing, invented by Pop Warner (along with the single-wing), positioned the quarterback behind a guard, and the snap went to the fullback. In youth ball, it must be simpler, and so the quarterback is under the center to take the snap. This offensive pattern provides for a greater level of misdirection-type play.

The *wing-T* is popular; its formation is like the T-formation, except one halfback plays out at a wing position, and the end on the other side is split out.

WHICH FORMATION SHOULD BE USED?

Each coach will have his own favorite formations. Your choice of formation depends on age and talent, and on how much time you are willing to put into it. The I-formation is quite popular, especially if you have a dominant running back. At beginner levels, the wishbone is a good choice since it's simpler. The double-wing involves misdirection and is a bit more advanced. I think you need to use at least two formations to keep the defense on its toes, so I recommend you start with the I-formation and wishbone formation at ages up to eleven. Add some power-I or slot-I plays as you go, and then experiment with the double-wing at older levels. Hundreds of different offensive plays can be run from the various formations. The key to success is to have a workable set of plays, perhaps fifteen of them, that the kids understand completely and can memorize against several defenses. Parents can help by quizzing their child on his plays. Coaches get very irritated when kids forget plays, which happens a great deal, and it has cost many boys their starting positions. But remember to be patient, especially those first couple of years. It takes a lot of practice for kids to learn and remember plays.

Players should know what *every* person should do on *every* play. At young ages, kids are often shifted to different positions, and a coach may make changes all season long. If he calls on a player to change position and the player has no idea how to play the new position, the kid will lose an important opportunity. It pays to understand the concept behind each play and what everybody has to do. At the very least, linemen should know what other linemen must do, backs other backs, and so on.

OFFENSIVE PLAY PATTERNS

The number of possible offensive plays is endless, but your players cannot memorize or effectively run very many. There are only six gaps to run through in the interior line. Add the two sweeps around the end, and you don't need a lot of plays to attack those holes. You will want to favor the side of your line where your best blockers are, so you only really need eight to ten running plays and five passing plays for your chosen primary formation. Your secondary formation can add a few more running plays, modified slightly to fit the formation, with no change to most blocking assignments.

A player must approach each play from the standpoint of the area he is to block. The defensive formation on the play diagram or the formation used in practice may change, or the defense may pull a stunt. Usually, at youth levels, the defense has a five- or six-man line with two linebackers. In the 5-2 defense, the nose guard lines up on the offensive center, the defensive tackles are on the outside shoulder of offensive tackles, the ends are outside the offensive end, and the linebackers are on the guards. However, sometimes a youth team uses a six-man defensive line, with linemen covering each gap. A player must understand that his assignment is to block *whomever* is in his area of responsibility, and that he needs to block them away from the path of the ball carrier. Obviously, he must also know where the ball carrier is going. A general understanding of the play will make him more valuable since he can react to changing circumstances if he knows the concept of the play.

OFFENSIVE NOMENCLATURE

Running plays are designed to run into the gaps between offensive linemen, which are called call *holes* and to which numbers are assigned. (See figure 5-10.) In addition, the running backs are numbered, with the quarterback as number 1, the fullback as number 3, the left halfback or tailback as number 2, and the right halfback or flankerback as number 4. The left end is assigned the letter X and the right end is assigned Y. Plays are coded to include these numbers; for instance, *31 Dive* signifies that the number 3 back (the fullback) will carry through the number 1 hole between the left guard and center and that blocking is straight ahead. The offensive formations are also given numbers,

5-10. HOLE NUMBERING AND BACKS/RECEIVERS DESIGNATIONS

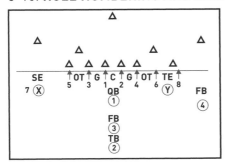

This numbering scheme is the most common and long-standing. Odd holes are on the left; even are on the right. Backs are numbered 1 through 4. Ends are designated X and Y.

such as number 1 for an I-formation right (flanker set to the right), number 2 for I-left, number 3 for wishbone, and so forth. For example, *131* means I –right, fullback, number 1 hole. Alternatively, the coach may elect to just use the actual words. Words take longer, using up the game clock, but are clearer. I like using numbers if the quarterback is allowed to change plays on the line of scrimmage.

FIVE KEY PLAY TYPES

There are categories, or types of plays, with specific patterns within each class. Look at the playbook on pages 104-112 to see how each play is run.

1. Up the middle. A *dive* is a run up the middle to either side of center; that is, into the number 1 or number 2 hole. It is a favorite of many coaches because it's so simple, but that's also its weakness. Because it is a quick play, there is no time to pull a guard or get a back to lead the play through the hole, so there is less force at the line than needed. The key to this play is its speed, and it works best if the ball is hiked on the first sound the quarterback makes. The running back must see the linebacker and try to head to the side where the blocker, usually a guard, is trying to drive him. This play can work with a good, strong center and guard. Run it to the side of the stronger guard.

A *blast* is a more effective play at youth levels. It uses a lead blocker (usually a fullback) out of a wishbone formation, leading the halfback. A *power play* uses two lead blockers, usually the fullback and a pulling guard. Another delayed dive is the *draw play*, where the quarterback drops back as if to pass. He quickly raises the ball in a passing stance, causing the linebackers to drop back, and then he hands off to a waiting running back. If the quarterback it is not convincing, it can lead to lost yardage. The *quarterback sneak* is a highly effective dive play in which the quarterback takes the snap and immediately drives forward to one side of the center. It is effective because the quarterback gets into the gap quickly, before the defense is fully prepared to tackle, and thus can usually get a yard or two. Frankly, it should be used more often than just to get a yard on a third-and-one situation.

2. Slants. A *slant* runs into the defensive line to the right or left side. It can be off-guard into the number 3 or number 4 hole. However, this play runs into the linebackers' strength, so unless you have a very good blocking guard or back, it's usually not a good choice. *Off-tackle* is another slant play into the number 5 or number 6 hole. It's used frequently, since the end of the defensive line is usually weaker than the middle, and since the offensive tackle is usually the strongest kid on the line. But the key here is the tight end. Ends at youth levels need to be chosen more for their blocking abilities than their catching abilities. Too often, coaches look for the pass catcher, forgetting how few passes are thrown. A good blocking end makes all the difference. These two players need to know their assignments against all defenses and stunts on this play and be ready for any of them. A *counter motion*—sending the running back in one direction, then having the halfback counter, come back the other way, and get the handoff—is often very effective at youth levels since weakside defenders often don't stay home, guarding against any misdirection. It's always useful to try to get the linebackers leaning the wrong way.

3. Wide plays. An *end-around* goes (you got it!) around the end into the number 7 or number 8 lane. The *sweep play* goes even wider, using the number 9 or number 10 lane. With a speedy running back, and a good blocking back and/or guard to lead the play, this is the most dangerous play in youth ball for the defense. If you have the fastest kid on the field, run it all day. It usually works best with a *pitchout* to the running back. In a pitchout, the halfback immediately heads toward the sideline and the quarterback turns and pitches the ball underhanded to him as he goes. A fake to a fullback diving into the line can also get defensive backs headed in the wrong direction. A crackback block on the defensive end by a split end or flanker will also help. A *reverse* is a very effective sweep play since the original misdirection gets everyone moving in one direction, and a wingback comes in to reverse the ball. It's important to have a quarterback who can lead the wingback and block the first defender coming in from the outside (defensive end or outside linebacker). A split end or wide receiver can also help spring the play with a good block.

4. Option plays. In an *option play*, the quarterback must decide whether to run with the ball or pitch it out to a trailing running back. In the play, the quarterback runs wide with another running back on his outside shoulder. It works best with a split end, who can crackback block on the defensive end. If a tackler (usually the defensive end or a containing linebacker) approaches, the quarterback has the option of 1) cutting inside if he sees a hole forming, 2) keeping the ball wide if the contain man is blocked, or 3) pitching the ball out to the other runner. I've also seen the *triple option play* in Pop Warner ball. Here, the quarterback turns to hand the ball to the fullback. However, he *rides the belly* of the fullback; that is, he holds the ball close to the fullback's midsection while looking at the defensive tackle before releasing the ball. If the tackle commits himself forward on the outside shoulder of his blocker, the quarterback releases the ball for the dive up the middle. If the tackle holds back, covering the inside zone, the quarterback takes the ball back, lets the fullback go by toward the line of scrimmage, and heads outside with a trailing halfback for a regular option pattern. More and more often, coaches are using plays that give options depending on what the defense does after the play starts.

5. Passing patterns. As noted, passing plays don't generally work well with kids. However, they should be practiced and can be useful with a little luck. Coaches call passing patterns by different names or numbers. Some use a *passing tree* concept to denote the various routes a runner may take. (See figure 5-11.) The receiver runs straight ahead, as if along a tree trunk from the roots upwards, and then cuts, like a branch, to the middle or toward the sideline. I like to see passing plays that mirror the receiver's normal blocking pattern on running plays. In this case, the receiver heads out like he is going to block, forearms out, and then breaks into open space. I also like passes across the middle. They are easier to throw and to catch, and they seem to work better in youth ball. An effective pass is the slant to a tight end, who simply slants at a 45-degree angle toward midfield, just behind the defensive line. The quarterback must release quickly on no more than a one-step drop back. The same pass cutting across the middle is called *underneath,* that is, between linebackers and defensive backs. A deeper pattern, maybe 10 yards deep, is *across the middle.* Of course, the *deep post patterns* are designed to get a lot of yards when needed, but a tall, agile receiver is a must. There are other several other passing plays, such as *buttonhooks,* where the receiver fakes deep and quickly stops and turns for the pass,

5-11. PASSING TREE

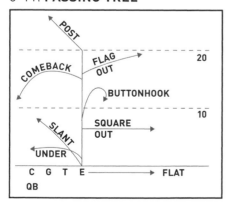

Like branches on a tree, this figure depicts the myriad routes a receiver can take. The number of possible routes is large and will vary depending on defensive coverage, but these are the key moves.

and *halfback option* passes, where the halfback fakes a run and then he passes to a receiver deep.

While it doesn't generally work well in youth football, a pass to the sideline can work in certain situations, such as where the defense has a very weak cornerback on one side. A short pass toward the sideline is called *out to the flat*, and it's usually to a wing or wide receiver who lines up on that side. If it's coupled with a fake running play into the line to pull in the cornerback, it often works well. A deeper pattern, maybe 10 yards deep and to the sideline, is a *side out*.

COACH'S PLAYBOOK

The series of diagrams that follow give a few dozen plays. Most are listed out of the I-formation, but can be easily converted to a wishbone. I show most plays against a 5-2 or a 6-2 defense. It's important for each coach to pick maybe eight to ten running plays and drill them to perfection. Then modify the plays based on your team's talent, experience, and scouting reports. Feel free to experiment; that's the fun of offensive coordination.

PLAY 1. **I-RIGHT, 32 DIVE**

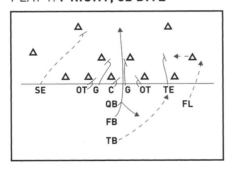 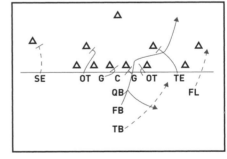

DEFENSE 5-2   **DEFENSE 6-2**

In this simple dive play, the fullback powers into the line. Blocking is headon, with the blocker's head to the playside of the defender. Go with a quick count; it's all about speed. It's not often successful unless you have a very good interior line. The fullback looks at the near linebacker, especially in a 6-2, and tries to use his blocker as a shield. **Play 2:** The opposite of this play is I-Left, 31 Dive.

PLAY 3. **I-RIGHT, 25 BLAST**

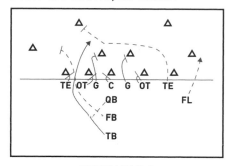

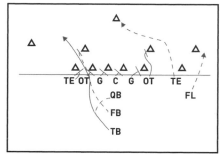

| DEFENSE 5-2 | DEFENSE 6-2 |

This is an off-tackle blast. The fullback leads the play and blocks the nearest defender in the hole. He may need to help out with the linebacker. The tailback looks for open space on either side of fullback. **Play 4:** The opposite of this play is I-Left, 26 Blast.

PLAY 5. **I-RIGHT, 26 SLANT, CROSS**

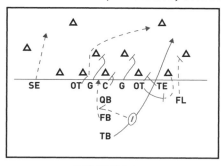

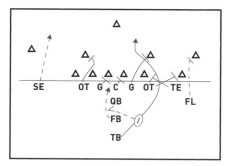

| DEFENSE 5-2 | DEFENSE 6-2 |

This off-tackle slant relies on a good fake to the fullback, diving left, to get the right linebacker leaning to his right, and a good cross-block on the defensive tackle and defensive end. **Play 6:** The opposite of this play is I-Left, 25, Slant, Cross.

PLAY 7. **I-RIGHT, 28 PITCH**

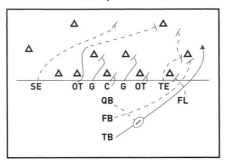

DEFENSE 5-2

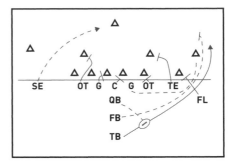

DEFENSE 6-2

This is a great play if you have a speedster. Practice the timing of the pitch so he doesn't lose a step. The flankerback needs to move quickly to avoid hitting the defensive end from behind. **Play 8:** The opposite of this play is I-Left, 27 Pitch.

PLAY 9. **I-RIGHT, 34 TRAP**

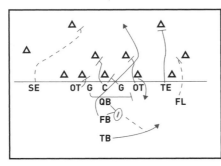

DEFENSE 5-2

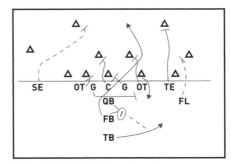

DEFENSE 6-2

The quarterback fakes a quick pitch to the tailback and spins to hand off to the fullback. The fullback keys off the back of the pulling guard, looking for a hole. **Play 10:** The opposite of this play is I-Left, 35 Trap.

PLAY 11. **I-RIGHT, 25 COUNTER**

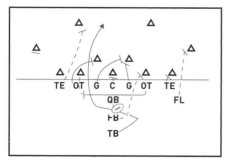

DEFENSE 5-2

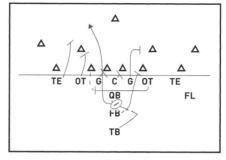

DEFENSE 6-2

Misdirection is set up by the tailback taking two steps right, as if he's following the fullback, then he counters toward the 5 hole, keying off the back of the pulling tackle. **Play 12:** The opposite of this play is I-Left, 24 Counter.

PLAY 13. **WISHBONE RIGHT, 17 TRIPLE LEFT**

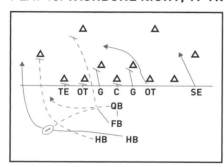

DEFENSE 5-2

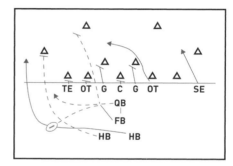

DEFENSE 6-2

Here's a triple option out of a wishbone: The quarterback, looking at what the defensive tackle does, bellies, that is, holds the ball near the fullback's belly. If the tackle is blocked, the quarterback gives the fullback the ball; otherwise, he sweeps out with the option of running through the 8 hole or pitching to the right halfback. **Play 14:** The opposite of this play is Wishbone Left, 18 Triple Right.

PLAY 15. **WISHBONE RIGHT, 3 Y REVERSE**

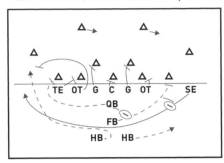

DEFENSE 5-2

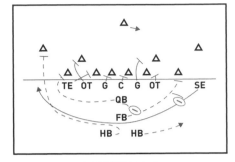

DEFENSE 6-2

It's razzle-dazzle time. The quarterback hands off to the fullback who is headed toward right end. The right split end must beat the defensive end to the fullback and get the handoff (Fullback blocks trailing defensive end). The left halfback takes two short, quick steps right and counters to lead the play left. The quarterback seeks out left defensive end. The right tackle takes a step right and loops around to get the left cornerback. The left end slant blocks the defensive tackle.

PLAY 16. **I-RIGHT, 4 Y SQUARE OUT**

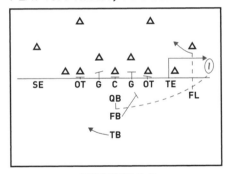

DEFENSE 5-2

This is a bread-and-butter play. The fullback dives toward the 4 hole, to pull in right side linebacker. The quarterback fakes a turn to hand off but quickly fires a dart to slanting tight end, who squares out underneath the flanker-back going deep.

PLAY 17. **I-RIGHT, 4Y SLANT**

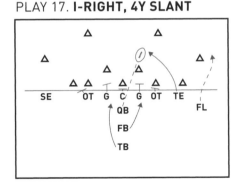

DEFENSE 6-2

This is a play-action fake to the fullback headed to the hole. And a quick pass to the slanting right tight end. The action needs to be quick.

PLAY 18. **I-RIGHT, 4 Y OUT, BOOTLEG**

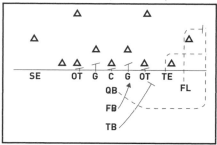

This is play action to the fullback headed toward the hole, and bootleg right. Look for tight end as a primary receiver, cutting under the right corner. Then look to the flankerback deeper at sideline.

PLAY 19. **I-RIGHT, X POST, 4 OUT**

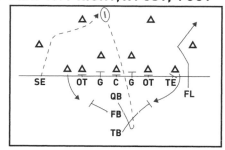

Here's a deep post pattern (toward the goal post); it's also known as a Hail Mary or deep bomb. They don't work very often, but on third and very long, there is not much choice.

PLAY 20. **I-RIGHT, 18-KEEP**

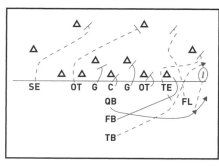

DEFENSE 5-2

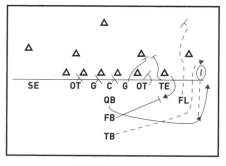

DEFENSE 6-2

This is a quarterback keeper, right. The flankerback heads deep trying to draw coverage. The tailback heads to the flat to block the cornerback. If he misses, he looks to the quarterback for a possible pass. Otherwise, the quarterback heads wide and turns the corner. **Play 21:** The opposite of this play is I-Left, 17-Keep.

PLAY 22. **I-RIGHT, TB PASS**

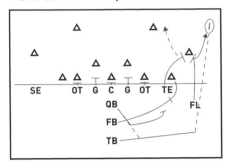
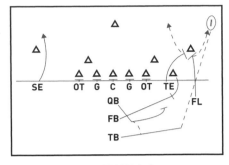

DEFENSE 5-2   **DEFENSE 6-2**

The tailback passes can work since kids are more easily faked at younger levels. Here the tight end and the flankerback both head to the cornerback, giving him a brief jolt, and then they split up into a pass pattern. The tailback looks to the sideline first, then to the tight end. **Play 23:** The opposite of this play is I-Left, TB Pass.

PLAY 24–25. **PUNT FORMATIONS**

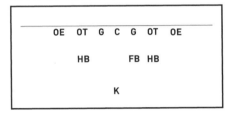
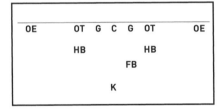

TIGHT FORMATION   **SPREAD FORMATION**

The tight formation is useful when the team is backed up near the end zone or if you have a poor snapper. Linemen are less than 2′ apart.

The spread formation looks for a snap at least 10 to12 yards, linemen can be 2 to 3 feet apart. In both formations, FB takes first player through up the middle, HBs take first through from their side.

110

PLAY 26–27. **KICKOFF FORMATIONS**

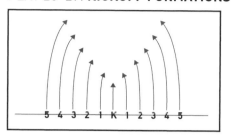

LANE COVERAGE

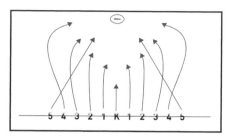

CROSS COVERAGE

Each player is assigned a lane and must protect it until it is clear the ball is going the other way. Then they angle to the ball carrier, still protecting their lane side of the ball.

In cross coverage, two speedsters on the side are released to hunt the ball if it comes down on their side. They have no lane coverage. The remaining players adjust to larger lanes. The kicker always acts as a safety, getting between the ball carrier and the goal.

PLAY 28-29. **KICKOFF RETURNS**

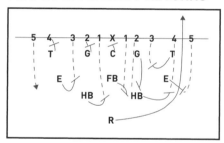

RIGHT WALL

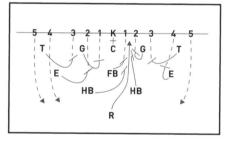

MIDDLE RUN

Players form a wall along the right side, wait until players approach their area, and then block. The rightside end takes #5 on far right and pushes him out of bounds.

On a middle return, each player is assigned a player on the other team except the two halfbacks who lead the play through the hole, either double-teaming the #1 and #2 opponent or the nearest opponent to the hole.

PLAY 30. **PUNT RETURN**

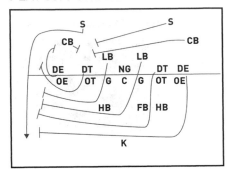

PLAY 31. **PLACE-KICK FORMATION**

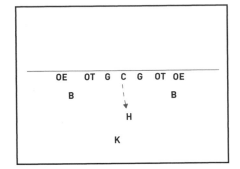

RIGHT WALL

All linemen head to the right side to form a wall. The right side hit their men and retreat immediately to the wall position. The left side attempt a blocked kick and then head to the assigned wall position. Other backs head to the receiver and take on the first tacklers to threaten them.

Linemen are shoulder to shoulder with no space between them at all. Wingbacks take on any outside rush.

112

DEFENSE: CONCEPTS AND FORMATIONS

06

A special feeling, a strong pride, comes from being a defensive ballplayer. The offensive backs may get more glory, but that stared to change when that great linebackers, such as Lawrence Taylor, paved the way to defensive recognition. I pointed out that the essence of football is the desire to overcome an opponent. Defense is made for this. Players have full use of the hands, whereas offensive players are significantly more constrained. Defense is blood-and-guts, clawing, scraping, head-knocking, gritty, thumping football! However, some general concepts find their way through all the sound and fury, and they are most helpful to understand. Talk these over with your players.

TOP TEN DEFENSIVE CONCEPTS

1. Look for keys that signal where the play will go. Defenders must always be sensitive to clues or hints as to where the play will go. However, the best defensive tool, particularly at the less-complicated youth level, is to play according to the motion or flow of the offense, focusing particularly on certain players such as the offensive guard. Here are some specific keys to look for and what they mean:

> a. If the guard does not charge forward but steps back a bit in a stationary position, he is pass-blocking, and it's a pass play.
>
> b. If the guard crosses the line of scrimmage, it's a running play, probably up the middle.
>
> c. If the guard pulls in either direction, it's a running play in that direction.
>
> d. If the guard's pads are low, suggesting he intends to drive forward and block, it's a run. If the pads are high, it signals he will step back to pass block, and so it's a pass play.

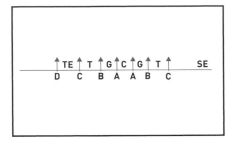

The defensive backs can generally rely on these keys to help them react quickly and know what type of play is coming. Obviously, they must keep one eye on the guard and one on the ball.

2. Plug the gaps. As with the numbering of offensive holes, the defense assigns letters to the gaps between offensive linemen. (See figure 6-1.) Controlling these gaps and penetrating through them, is the prime objective of defensive strategy. The offense can't run where there is no hole. Some defenses, using an eight-man front, try to assign a player to every gap. Of course, this focuses on the run and exposes the defense to passing threats, with only man-to-man coverage at best. The five- or seven-man front relies on the nose tackle to cover both gaps on either side of center. If you have a dominant nose guard, try it. Most often, the eight-man defense is needed to control the run, especially in short-yardage situations or on a first down. A defensive player's options include playing *head-on* a blocker, *shading* his blocker's inside or outside shoulder, or shooting the middle of the gap between the offensive linemen. I've even seen complex numbering schemes that further dissect a gap into three areas; each area of each gap has a distinct number, called a *technique*. This occurs more at high-school or college levels. At youth levels, players are usually head-on a blocker, in defenses such as a 5-2, or responsible for a gap in defenses such as a 6-2.

3. Go with the flow. The flow of a play is usually instantly revealed. The whole team suddenly shifts one way or the other, and the defense must respond immediately. The offensive line's first two steps are the most critical. Watch the linemen, not the backs, since a pulling or slanting lineman will almost always signal that the play is in that direction. The defense should try to get in front of the flow, thus reducing advantage of surprise that comes with the offense's knowledge of the timing of the snap. Of course, misdirection, fakes, and razzle-dazzle all require that the defense keeps their eyes on the ball and not just on the flow. But the flow of offensive linemen is usually a great indicator of the play.

4. Pressure the middle. An offensive team that can drive up the middle for 4 or 5 yards each play will dominate the game and keep the other team's offense off the field. It follows that a key job of the defense is to shut down the power running game. Youth teams put their strongest players up the middle on defense. Once the defense bangs back a few offensive dives, the offense will be forced to go to less successful plays like sweeps or passes. It's easier to stop a sweep or pass since they are more complicated to execute, and therefore the defense has time to get more people on the job. The offense has to rely on skillful execution to pull off wide plays. However, up the middle is considered power territory. The team that controls the middle of the line has a decided advantage. I believe, since youth ball has such a dominant running game, that an eight-man defensive front of six linemen and two linebackers—all assigned to gaps—is most effective.

5. Contain and force the play inside. In soccer, the ball is forced outside, wide away from the goal. In football, however, the objective is to keep the runner inside where there is always more defensive help. Whatever defense you use, there is always a *contain man*, someone seeking to contain a run and turn it inside. We also call this *facing space,* that is, the open space of the flat, outside the offensive end, ready to penetrate forward a few feet, turn in to face the middle, and contain, letting nothing get past him to the outside. The primary job of the defensive end—or outside linebacker or cornerback, depending on the formation—is to turn the wide running play inside. Cornerbacks likewise are told to approach the man from the outside and turn him in where teammates are hopefully in pursuit. Most big gains on running plays happen when a back somehow gets by the outside man and sprints down the sideline.

If a team has a speedster, the end must not let him run around him. It is critical for your contain man, the defensive end or an outside linebacker, to hold his ground and keep the play inside him. If the defensive end goes for a fake running play into the line and begins to pursue that play, the sweep will gain a lot of yardage. Contain players must know when it's their responsibility to contain and must hold that outside position until it is clear that the ball will not come their way. If the sweep comes at them, they must ride their blocker along the line of scrimmage, forcing the play wider while waiting for help.

6. Stay home. One of the biggest problems with youth defenses is a tendency to abandon a key coverage and go with the flow too much. I recall a game in high school where our defensive end, who had outside containment responsibility (which meant

115

that his job was to *not* allow the ball to get around his end), just could not resist the urge to follow a fullback into the line. The quarterback made a great fake to him. In the films the next day it was almost funny to see the defensive end turn around and quizzically watch as the halfback carrying the ball ran around the end, untouched, for a touchdown. Another defensive mistake that often occurs is when a linebacker covering the middle abandons his position, leaving the whole midfield open, which allows the quarterback to scramble out of danger, up the middle, and gain yards. This does not mean that a player shouldn't leave to pursue the ball; it just means he cannot do so unless it's clear the play will not come back his way.

7. Keep the pursuit. Kids must be told to keep moving until the whistle blows. If the play goes the other way, they must chase it—laterally at first to ensure against a reverse. Then they must head downfield at an angle that seems reasonable and run until they hear a whistle. How often during a youth game do you see defensive personnel stopped, standing upright, watching a play that goes to the opposite side? It causes me to wonder whether coaches at youth levels teach this concept. I know when I played that the instinct to take a little rest when the action went the other way was quite strong. However, many times the action will turn back to the middle, and thus pursuing the ball carrier can lead to a big tackle and save a touchdown. Furthermore, the play could turn to the far corner and a pursuing defender can often take an angle to meet the runner downfield.

Of course, a defender cannot get into pursuit if he is entangled with his blocker. This is why it is so important to keep the blocker away from the body, using the hands to push or shiver him away, then shed him and engage in pursuit of the ball carrier. Good pursuit wins close games.

8. Confuse the offense with stunts and blitzes. Defensive linemen and linebackers have a certain *zone*, or gap, to defend. But, sometimes their primary positions are changed to confuse offensive blocking assignments. A *stunt* is a defensive play in which responsibilities are swapped. A defensive tackle, usually responsible for the outside shoulder area of his opponent, slants diagonally inside, while the inside linebacker loops around him to cover the off-tackle play. (See figure 6-2 on page 117.)

Stunts can confuse offensive blockers and often result in easy tackles. However, a slip-up here can also play into the hands of the offense. The tackle could get blocked on a dive up the middle, and the linebacker will have taken himself out of the play.

Another stunt that is often very effective is the *blitz*. One or more backs in the defensive secondary leave their positions and crash forward into the line. This play

6-2. STUNTS

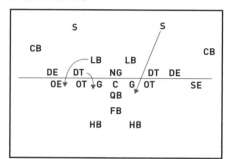

Two stunts are presented here. On the left, a tackle and linebacker exchange positions, the tackle slanting in and the linebacker looping around. On the right, a safety blitz occurs through the inside tackle hole.

is often successful, confusing blockers and resulting in quick tackles and a loss of yardage. It is usually employed during a passing down, such a third down and ten, when the quarterback will need to hold the ball a bit longer to allow his receivers to go deep. The extra time allows the blitzing defenders to get to the quarterback. However, a substantial number of times, it will backfire. With fewer defensive backs left to cover receivers, they can get open for the pass. Or, if a running play was called through a gap different from the one the defense targets, the ball carrier will face fewer defenders if he makes it into the secondary. A big gain of yards, or even a score, is possible. Stunts can work both ways, but more often they work very well for the defense.

9. Remember pass defense. The three keys to pass defense are: 1) hold the receivers; 2) rush (or pressure) the passer; and 3) get the ball. It's unfortunate that pass defense has such a low priority at the youth levels since there are so few passes. But against a passing team, and certainly in high school, pass defense fundamentals are essential to stopping the aerial game.

The first key in pass defense is to delay the receivers at the line of scrimmage for a step or two. Any delay in running their patterns takes precious time from the quarterback and adds substantially to the pressure on him. Pressure on a quarterback produces more errant passes than anything else. On a passing down, the defensive end gives a shoulder or forearm to the offensive end to delay him. A cornerback shivers a wide receiver at the line of scrimmage for a second. A second is all that is needed. The defensive back can hit a receiver only in the first 5 yards, by rule, and cannot touch him after that. It's also important not to hold the receiver, which is a serious penalty. However, it is helpful to delay him for a step or two, even if only by getting in his way.

6-3. **PRESSURE THE QUARTERBACK**

Successful passes under pressure rarely are made.

The second key is to pressure the passer. If the quarterback has four or five seconds to throw the ball, he can pass at will. Time gives receivers a real advantage to change direction, make fakes, and break free. When the defensive line sees a pass play developing (it becomes evident quickly that it is a pass play when the offensive linemen do not cross the line of scrimmage), they must engage in a furious and frantic penetration to the quarterback. Nothing is more unsettling to a quarterback than to be under pressure. (See figure 6-3.) Pressure is the best weapon against passing accuracy, and a quarterback sack gives a decided momentum to the defensive team. Kids should be instructed to yell "Pass!" as soon as they see a pass play develop. This word should act as a lightning bolt to the defensive line to *charge*, or rush, the passer. Just the sound of their frenzy can be upsetting to the quarterback.

The third key is to get the ball. Once the ball is in the air, it is anybody's ball. As long as the defender is going for the ball, he has as much right to it as the intended receiver. Therefore, once the ball is airborne, the defense should go for it. A defender can forget the receiver if he has a chance to intercept the pass. Otherwise, the defender must time his approach to hit the receiver as soon as he catches the ball. Anticipation is the defenseman's best friend. He should lash at the ball to jar it free and, if a teammate makes the interception, the defensive player should not hesitate to block for him immediately.

10. Pay attention to down and distance. The defensive strategy varies with the down and the distance. On a short yardage play, throw eight players into every gap and have the defensive backs key on the ball carrier, that is, focus on him instead of potential receivers in an effort to stop the run up the middle. However, on long yardage, loosen up to a 5-2, or even a 4-4 defense. Allow a short pass in front of your defense, that is, short of a the first down line. However, the primary job of the defensive secondary is to never let a receiver beat them deep. They should give up the short pass rather than allow a deep pass to succeed.

DEFENSIVE PASS COVERAGE

This is one of the most difficult areas to coach. Only one out of ten plays, at best, is a pass play. The easy solution at youth levels is to tell defensive backs to find the ball and go to it … period. However, they must learn to protect against the occasional pass. They do so by watching the quarterback, watching the flow of the offense, and listening to the linebackers. If it looks like a pass, they must react and fall into pass coverage.

I like a combination of man-to-man and zone coverage on defense. One linebacker is responsible for the middle of the field at all times. Perhaps he is the middle linebacker, or the linebacker not blitzing or stunting in a 6-2 defense. Someone must always be responsible for the midfield area on a pass play. Whoever that is covers the whole midfield area, looking for receivers cutting across the middle. He looks at the quarterback's eyes and his motion to help tip off where the pass may go. He also stays home to cover any scramble or screen. The linebackers key on certain runners, with the strongside linebacker focusing on the primary running back, or tailback, and the weakside keying on the blocking back. On a pass play, they follow these players if they go out for a pass, usually a short pass to the flat.

The defensive cornerbacks all go to man-to-man coverage, staying with the first receiver in their area, usually a split end or wide receiver. The safety is a jack of all trades, responsible for the deep pattern, assisting the corner with a deep pass or covering the cornerback's man if a second man comes into the corner area. He also covers the middle zone and picks up the first receiver to come across the middle behind the linebackers. Most youth passing plays send one to three men into patterns, so the three or four defensive secondary players cover them.

DEFENSIVE FORMATIONS

The idea on defense is to keep enough strength up the middle to force the offense to run wide or pass. Success up the middle is critical to winning football games. A good middle or inside linebacker is the most critical position to defensive success. I've also seen good nose guards terrify the offense, cause mis-snaps and fumbles, unnerve the quarterback, and generally wreak havoc in the offensive backfield.

Not as many defensive formations are employed as offensive formations, particularly at the young ages. The standard high-school defense is a five-man line with two inside linebackers, two cornerbacks, and two deep safeties. The four-man defensive line is used more in professional ball where there is more passing. (See figure 6-4 on page 121.) In short-yardage situations, a team goes to a six- or seven-man defensive line, plus linebackers. The eight-man gap defense is used on goal-line situations. I prefer the 6-2 defense as a general defensive setup for kids. It seems to provide the balance needed for the youth running game. However, if you have a very dominant nose guard who can reliably cover both gaps around center, then a 5-2 is available to you.

The 6-2. This is a solid youth defense, yielding essentially an eight-man line with the six down linemen and the two linebackers. Each lineman is responsible for a gap, usually the same gap each play, unless they are stunting with a linebacker, in which case they *shoot*, or penetrate, the gap normally assigned to the linebacker. If not stunting, the linebackers can focus on a runner. The side of the offensive formation with more players on it is called the strongside. Usually the strongside linebacker keys on the tailback or primary running back, and the weakside will key on a blocking back. Each linebacker will be responsible for the midfield on a play flowing away from his side, and so he must "stay home."

The cornerbacks have contain responsibility and must force plays inside. Likewise, the defensive ends penetrate and try to force the play inside. On a passing play, all linemen rush the quarterback and look for an opportunity to get their hands up into a passing lane by looking at the quarterback's motion. Linebackers cover short passes in their zone, which is the first 10 yards on their side of the line of scrimmage, and key on the first player into the short zone. Cornerbacks take the first man into their area and stay with him deep. The free safety moves laterally toward the deepest player, allowing no one deeper than himself in the middle third of the field.

6-4. DEFENSIVE FORMATIONS

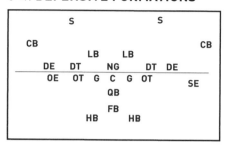

The 5-2. This is the standard defense at the youth level, and you will see a lot of it. It's been called the Oklahoma 54, which includes the cornerbacks, but it's really a seven-man line, with five down linemen and two linebackers. It nicely balances against the run and the pass and equally distributes individual defensive responsibility across the line with defenders generally hitting gaps. I like the 6-2 better, but would use the 5-2 for long yardage plays.

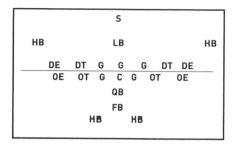

The Seven Diamond. This is also called the seven gap since most linemen are in gaps. It's a short-yardage defense with heavy responsibility on the halfbacks. The middle linebacker taps the nose guard to let him know which gap to go to, and the linebacker covers the other gap. It's really an eight-man line.

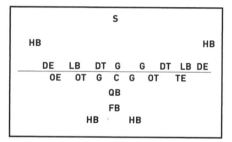

The Goal Line. In this formation every gap is plugged, all eight are down linemen, and the three defensive backs must assist by stopping the ball at the line.

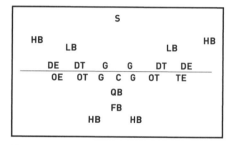

The 6-2. A six-man line, stronger against the run than the 5-2, especially off-tackle. I believe this is the right defensive formation for kids, particularly at first down, or any down with less than 8 yards to go.

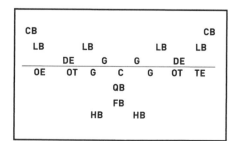

The Four-Man Line. In this formation every gap is covered, essentially an eight-man line, and the three defensive backs must assist by stopping the ball at the line.

07 RUNNING TEAM PRACTICES

A major factor as to why some teams improve during a season and others don't is how effective practices are, and this depends on how well organized the coach is. Practices are essential to improve form, skills, execution and timing of plays, and overall teamwork. Practices also toughen kids up. However, far too often we see kids standing around at practices, wasting precious time and learning opportunities. Being organized will save time and maximize practice opportunities. You must have a plan for each practice. Write it out, and make sure it keeps the team busy.

PRE-SEASON PREPARATION

Perhaps the most common question from parents who begin to coach a team in any sport is, "How do I start?" or "How do I run a practice?" The job starts early. A month or so before the first practice, you should communicate with your team, and especially with parents, on a number of matters.

Football requires strength and endurance, and players will have a much easier start if they show up in decent shape. It's best if players are able to do at least six 20-yard wind sprints, fifteen to thirty push-ups, and twenty-five to fifty sit-ups. This will ensure that the legs, upper body, and trunk are in reasonable condition. The kids should work at least every other day for a month to get up to this level. Parents can work out with them to get exercise, too.

Players and parents need to know that practices are important and that being on time is critical for them and for the team. The game schedule, practice schedule, and starting and ending times should be communicated as soon as available so parents can begin arranging for transportation, etc.

You should also communicate that you welcome help. At least three assistant coaches are needed and four or five is better: two for offense, with one for line, and one for backs;

two for defense, with one for line, and one for backs; and one for special teams. A team parent or two is needed to help with incidentals, uniforms, candy drives, organizing car pools, and keeping stats at games. Ask for help. A sample letter to parents follows.

Dear Parent/Guardian,

Welcome to the *(Name)* Football program. Our season begins in five weeks, and I'd like to go over a few things that will help us get off to a great start!

Practices will start on August 1, and we will have practice, Monday to Friday evenings, until school starts. We may have a few weekend scrimmages, and I'll let you know the dates as soon as I have them. We'll practice for two hours each evening, from 6 to 8 P.M. During the school season, we'll practice three times a week, on Tuesday, Wednesday, and Friday, from 6 to 8 P.M. (or dusk). Games are on Sundays at 1 P.M., beginning September 5. It's important that your child arrives on time (a few minutes early is fine) and is picked up on time. Unless told otherwise, full gear is required at all practices. We will hand it out at the first practice, so just have them wear shorts or sweat pants at that practice. Kids should bring water bottles and a small towel.

It would be very helpful to your child to do some conditioning before the season starts so that initial practices are not too tiring. Jogging (up to a half mile), wind sprints (six for 20 yards each), push-ups (build up to at least fifteen to thirty), and sit-ups (twenty-five to fifty) are fine. *(For beginners or flag teams, you can cut the number of push-ups and sit-ups in half)*.

I promote parental involvement, and I need a few assistant coaches. Don't worry about experience. We can learn as we go. There is a great book called *Coaching Youth Football: The Guide for Coaches, Parents and Athletes* by John P. McCarthy, and I recommend you obtain it. I also need a team parent or two to help organize things. If you are interested, give me a call or see me at the first practice.

My philosophy is to help your child learn the skills and fundamentals to become better at and have fun with the great game of football. Every child will play in every game *(state the league rule about minimum number of plays)*. Those who work harder will get additional playing time, but they must earn it! Winning is fun, but it is not more important than making this a positive learning experience.

I hope you will keep this in mind when rooting for the team and your child at games. It's helpful to praise good hustle and effort, but it's not helpful to give specific instructions to your child during play (that's my role), or to comment on referee calls (they are learning, too). I will not allow criticism from parents or from other players.

It is most helpful for parents to work with their child at home to improve skills. Practice definitely leads to improvement, and so more is always better! Of course, if your schedule does not permit the above, you have already taken a big step by allowing your child to be involved and by providing transportation.

Please send me your e-mail address to facilitate quick communication. My e-mail is *(insert your e-mail address)*. Welcome aboard!

Best Regards,

Your Name
Phone number, address, and e-mail

EQUIPMENT

Most leagues will supply the full uniform for each player, except for shoes. In my area the kids pay a hundred bucks with their application to play, and put in a fifty dollar uniform deposit. The league will also have a primary practice field with a storage shed or building to keep practice equipment. They will usually have a six- to seven-man blocking sled, and a couple two-man sleds, as well various as blocking pads and shields and dummy pads. These are the essentials, and the market also has other coaching aides available to leagues. Several teams will share the practice field, and they will schedule sled practice at different times or days so all teams get to use it. It works out pretty well with some reasonable coordination and planning.

A high-school football must be four-paneled, pebble-grain, tan cowhide with eight or twelve evenly spaced laces. It should be 10⅞ to 11⁷⁄₁₆ inches long with a 20¾ to 21¼ inch middle circumference and a 27¾ to 28½ inch long circumference. It must weigh 14 to 15 ounces and be inflated to 12½ to 13½ pounds per square inch. At youth levels, the ball can be a bit smaller in most dimensions. Thus, the length can be 10 to 11 inches, the middle circumference can be 19 to 20 inches, the long circumference can be 26 to 27 inches, the weight can be 12 to 14 ounces, and inflation can be 12½ to 13½ pounds per square inch.

Pop Warner and National Federation rules require a helmet certified by the National Operating Committee on Standards for Athletic Equipment (NOCSAE) with a visible warning label, a properly fastened chin strap, a multiple-bar face protector of nonbreakable material, shoulder pads, hip pads with tailbone protector, thigh guards, kneepads, and mouth guard with a keeper strap, and an athletic supporter. I recommend that players wear a cup, sanctioned forearm pads and shin guards, and neck braces, even though they are not currently required. Kids may not wear any hard substance, such as a cast or knee brace, unless the hard surface is covered by ½-inch thick, closed cell, slow recovery rubber.

REINFORCE THE BASICS

The main thing kids need is to learn the basics of the game. Unlike other sports, it's not likely that beginners will have played any football, so you shouldn't assume too much. The kids need to know the various positions, the rules, and the basic skills. Spend a few minutes each practice at the outset going over the terms. Have a few new words each practice and ask the kids to tell you what they mean. Start with the basic stuff, such as parts of the field, rules, and positions. Make it fun and use the opportunity to elaborate on the meaning of things. If you have an older team with a few beginners, find a way to help the beginners understand the language of football. Tell parents to read this book. It's written for parents and grandparents as much as for coaches, and they can be a great help to you if they get involved early on in explaining the game and instructing their children.

HAVE A PLAN

There are several key objectives that you need to consider for each week's practice plan. Their relative importance will vary as you get further into the season, and they also vary depending upon the age group you work with, but these concepts are important and should be part of your plan for each practice.

1. Get the players in shape.
2. Understand each player's potential.
3. Work on individual skills for each position.
4. Work on team execution of plays.

Football practices typically last around two to two-and-a-half hours. All four objectives should be considered when you prepare a practice plan (I'll get to what a practice plan looks like a bit later). In a typical practice, I would devote thirty minutes to stretching and conditioning, thirty minutes to an hour to individual skills development, and one hour to team dynamics. Early in the season, you should spend more time on conditioning, speed, and agility drills; later in the season, spend more time on teamwork.

Let's discuss each practice objective.

1. Get the players in shape—thirty minutes per practice. It is of little use if players know their plays and have good timing, if they to run out of gas in the second half of a game. Frankly, it doesn't take much to get grade-school kids into shape, and there is no excuse when they aren't. The worst mistake is to assume that the kids will get themselves into shape. I knew a coach with a potential championship team who refused to spend time at practice on conditioning. His team never came close to success. By the same token, you can waste precious practice time by focusing too much on conditioning. A rigorous practice plan will keep players moving and get them conditioned as well.

Make sure players stretch and warm up before practice. A lap or two around the field at a slow pace should create a sweat and warm up the major leg muscles. Tell your players that muscles are like bubble gum—unless they stretch slowly, they will tear. (See figure 7-1.)

Don't expect that players will warm up sufficiently on their own. Tell them to do some calisthenics before practice starts, such as what I call the *Quick Cali Set*: twenty jumping jacks, twenty push-ups, fifteen partial sit-ups (bend the knees, bring the shoulder blades off the ground), twenty trunk turns, and five neck bridges (to do a neck bridge, kids lie on their back, arch the back up, and support the weight with the head and the heels of the feet). Start off very slow with light neck pressure. Kids can do these on their own; it takes just a few minutes.

7-1. TEAM LAP

A lap around the field at the start and finish of practice is great for conditioning.

126

Then call the team together for stretching. Stretching is critical, and you must ensure they do the stretches properly. Start with what I call the *Stretch Set*. These stretches should be done smoothly without jerking or straining. The first three are the best and should be done at every practice. I do them every time I work out.

1. **Hand-to-toe**. Sitting on ground with legs outstretched, reach and touch the toe with opposite hand; if the ground is wet, stand with feet crossed, bend over, and hold the stretch. Alternate from one foot to the other. (See figure 7-2.)
2. **Butterfly**. Sitting on the ground with knees outstretched and soles of the shoes touching, slowly move the knees toward the ground to stretch the inner thigh. Hold for fifteen seconds and repeat three times.
3. **Achilles and calf stretch**. Place one foot about a yard in front of the other. Lean forward and bend the front leg, stretching the lower part of the back leg. Reverse and do four repetitions for each leg. Don't use jerking movements or bob up and down.
4. **Supine hamstring**. Lying on the back, pull one leg to an upright straight position. Hold for ten seconds, then reverse legs. Repeat three times.
5. **Standing quadriceps**. Standing on one foot, grasp the other foot behind the back and gently pull it to the buttocks. Reverse. Do three for each leg.
6. **Thigh stretch**. Standing with legs outstretched, slowly lean to one side and bend that leg, stretching the under-thigh of the other leg. Do three for each leg.

The team captain can lead the stretching exercises. Let him start while you get organized, check to see who is there, or talk to your coaches and parents.

It's important to monitor your players. Evaluate the temperature at all times when doing conditioning and make sure none of the players get heat exhaustion, especially

7-2. **HAND-TO-TOE**

A: Sitting.　　　　　　　　　　　　　　B: Standing.

early in the season when it's hot and they are out of shape. (Monitor it for the whole practice on hot days.) On hot days, I prefer multiple, brief breaks instead of one ten-minute, mid-practice break.

Don't overwork your players. Some coaches have their kids running all the time, all season long. The players are young, but there are limits even for the young. By the same token, there will be periods when players are just standing around. I believe that push-ups are the best single exercise for building upper-body strength in kids (along with sit-ups). Assign sets of twenty push-ups or sit-ups freely. Tell the kids that it's not punishment. Tell them you are trying to give them an edge that they will need when they come up against their opponents. If a kid does a hundred push-ups a day, he will become quite strong. Judge what a player can do, and slightly push his limit. Don't ask him to do something that will embarrass him, though.

Speed and agility drills are also quite effective. Avoid wind sprints at the beginning of practice. They require loose muscles, so they should normally be done at the end. Do short ones, 5 to 10 yards at first, then 25 yards. Tell the players to reach out in a long stride. Run some backward and sideways. Finish with a few 25-yard races with players of the same position competing against each other—linemen, ends and fullbacks, then backs.

You can't do much to make a slow kid into a speedster. But you can improve speed somewhat, and you can improve running strength, agility, and balance a good deal. The following are drills to improve speed and agility. I'd avoid spending too much practice time on them. Use them to fill in a down period for some players, or focus them on players who are slow and clumsy. Urge players to do them at home.

Some good drills to improve running speed and form are:

1. **The Robot**. Line up players and have them run 40 yards at half speed, driving their fists down from neck height to just behind the buttocks. The idea is to bang or hammer the fists downward in a robotic cadence in rhythm with their stride. Have them run it three times, increasing speed each time.

2. **The Bounce**. This is similar to the drill above, except have them concentrate on lifting their knees high to the chest, bouncing off the ground with each step and lifting the knees as high as possible. After awhile, try to incorporate the first drill with the second.

3. **The Buttkick**. This is a great drill, universally used in football. Players run 40 yards kicking the heels into the buttocks.

4. **The Goosestep**. Finally, players run 40 yards in the old Russian or German military march, kicking the legs straight out and lifting them straight and high.

Some good drills to improve agility are:

1. **Simon Says**. Line up players in five lines. The first row of five starts to run in place, using short, quick, choppy steps. The coach signals with his hand, usually with a football in hand, to the players to shuffle laterally (without crossing the feet), then forward, then backward, then down to the ground and up again. Players must square the shoulders, stay low, and reach quickly. Slow reacting players who don't appear to be trying hard enough may be rewarded with a dozen push-ups.

2. **Carioca**. Line up as above. Players "carioca," that is, run sideways, left foot over right, then left foot behind right, for 40 yards. Repeat four times.

3. **Rope Drill**. Most clubs will have a rope drill set up. Players start at one end and quickly move to the other end, stepping forward into each square, trying not to get tripped up. (See figure 7-3.) You can make your own with 150 feet of rope and 100 feet of small PVC pipe with eight three-port, three-dimensional couplings and eight to twelve T-couplings. Assemble the PVC into two rectangles, 15 to 20 feet by 8 feet. Connect these two structures at each corner and in two or three points along the long side using six or eight 8- to 10-inch pipes. The height of these riser pipes can vary, depending on the size of your team. Enough supports are needed along the long side to avoid sagging. PVC is cheap and easy to cut. Attach and tape the rope to form two parallel rows of boxes; each box should be 18 inches long. As players hop-step through the boxes, tell them to stay low, lift their legs, and remain balanced.

Every practice should include a few drills from each category, including stretches, then speed and agility drills. Finish up the conditioning session with a lap around the field.

7-3. ROPE DRILL

Players move through the rope apparatus much like kids playing hopscotch, except as fast as they can. Time their speed with a stopwatch. This drill is great for agility and conditioning.

2. Understand each player's potential. You need to figure out pretty quickly what each player is capable of doing so that each can concentrate on developing the specific skills for his position. Then you should keep an open mind, and figure out which players you were wrong about. I've seen many coaches assign positions quickly and then never change their minds. I was an offensive end early in high school. One day, my coach saw me knock a few players down-and-quickly moved me to what was my natural position, offensive tackle. While it's important to get things set early so you can concentrate on the special skills required for each position (as discussed in chapter three), you should always be looking to see if a kid can better help the team somewhere else. Kids change from year to year, so don't base decisions exclusively on last year's performance. Assistant coaches can help you a lot here.

A good tool for understanding the potential of your players is to start making lists. Run sprints to evaluate the fastest players. Rank them by speed over 30 yards. Who can accelerate the fastest (short-distance speed)? Who is the most agile? Who are the gutsiest players? Who are the strongest players? Who has the best hands? Who are natural leaders? Make another list of every kid's name and write down each one's best attributes. Once you create these lists, don't throw them away. Check them every couple of weeks to see if someone has earned another look.

The lists are helpful since they focus on different aspects of athletic ability. Periodically reevaluate your players. It's incredible that some coaches rarely sit with assistant coaches to discuss each player. An assistant coach usually has seen something that can surface in a full review. Don't label a kid for the whole season. Reconsider frequently. Give a player a shot at something else if he is not working out where you first placed him.

You will find many brief opportunities on the practice field to talk to your players. "How is school?" "How are things at home?" "What are your interests?" You can find out a lot about a kid in just a few minutes to help you understand the player, and you will also begin to earn his respect. Kids who like and respect you are more coachable. You are a role model, so think about the messages you send by how you act.

3. Work on individual skills—thirty to sixty minutes per practice. After thirty minutes of stretching, warm-ups, and some speed and agility drills, call the players together. Tell them what they will be doing next and what you expect of them. Details can be supplied by assistant coaches later. Ask for their best effort at all times on the field. Talk about increasing the desire to overcome their opponents. Talk to beginners about the jargon of football. Chat about last week's game.

You should now focus on skills and fundamentals for each position. I think it's a great idea to film kids at practice. Try to get parent volunteers to take some shots of players working on form, either blocking against the sled or dummy pads, running play patterns, or pass catching. Do the linemen one day and the backs another. Circulate the tapes during the week to kids who need to see what they are doing wrong. Perhaps the line coach or the backs coach can meet some of the players at someone's house to view the films and talk about form. In coaching, a picture is truly worth a thousand words.

Your linemen need to work repeatedly on their form. If you have enough coaches to split them into offensive and defensive linemen, do so when needed to focus on particular skills, but both offensive and defensive skills need to be learned and practiced by all linemen.

For **offensive linemen**, the stance, charge, and jolt, as well as pulling and specialty blocks, should be demonstrated and reviewed. Look at the drills listed in chapter four, such as the Down-Set-Hut Drill, Timing Drill, Dummy Drill, and Unirail. After you (or the line coach) discuss with the players the fundamentals of blocking and demonstrate the correct form to them, have the players demonstrate the form back to you against dummy pads or a blocking sled. (See figure 7-4 A, B, C on page 132.) Have the checklist from chapter ten handy and see what needs to be adjusted. Make notes on each player so you know what changes need to be made in blocking form and work at each practice until the form is right. Keep working to maintain good form. If the player knows about your list, and that you will be looking at a specific part of his form at each practice, he will make it a priority. The concept of jolting can be practiced on dummies or on blocking sleds. Tell kids if they've given the sled a good shot. Get players in the habit of trying to get the sled to jolt. Have everyone listen for the "pop" that accompanies a good charge and jolt. Go over the checklist at the end of this book with coaches and players.

Too often, I see assistant coaches standing around, saying or doing little. They should be looking at each player and insisting on proper form. Working on form and fundamentals against dummy pads or sleds is essential. This must be done a few times a week. Good form goes a long way. If the head goes down, or the back curves, or if the legs stop driving or don't stay wide, let the player know. There is no excuse for poor form. A player may not be able to overcome an opponent, or execute every play well, but he can always employ proper form. Moreover, practice against sleds is the best method to strengthen legs and increase driving power.

Some of the best drills for linemen are done against a sled. If you have one available, it will help your players immensely. On sled drills, look for explosion, drive, jolt,

7-4. **BLOCKING FORM**

A: Mold the stance of each player until it is automatic for him.

B: Demonstrate the defensive shiver form against dummy pads.

C: Encourage them to pop the sled hard, low, and balanced.

and follow-through, with feet pumping all the time. Have the checklist handy to check out form. Agility can be added to the drill by having the players pop one pad and roll off to pop the next pad. If you don't have access to a sled, use dummy pads or standing dummy bags. Two players holding one bag can put up a lot of resistance, thus simulating the resistance of a sled.

Defensive linemen need to work on their fundamentals. They should work on the defensive stance, shivers, sheds, and other defensive fundamentals, while offensive linemen work on their form. The defensive stance is a bit different. Also, defensive linemen need to work on exploding off the snap, so use the timing drills mentioned in chapter four, such as the Form Drill, On the Ball Drill, Hold'm Drill, Bull in the Middle, and Pick a Lane. Have four or five linemen charge at each snap to see who gets off the fastest each time. Congratulate that player. Practice shiver thrusts against a sled or against dummy pads, and practice tackling against the sled or dummy bags. Discuss the fundamentals of shedding. Review how to look for the keys that reveal the coming offensive play.

I believe it's good to spend as much time as needed practicing fundamentals and form for **all linemen**. You should reserve about thirty to sixty minutes of practice for fundamentals, form, and sled practice. Twice a week, you should spend this time in a live, contact drill. These drills are just as effective and much safer when practicing at half or three-quarter speed to focus on form. Match players as evenly as possible when full speed. Let each play go for three seconds, then blow the whistle. Remember, you are looking for form improvement as well as infusing the desire to overcome the opponent. Don't use more than two players at a time—you want to be able to coach each player. Pit two offensive linemen, a yard apart, against a defensive lineman, who must go in between and through them. Practice pass blocking drills one-on-one or two-on-two.

Another good drill is one that anticipates defensive stunts. Pit one side of the offensive line (center-guard-tackle) against the corresponding defensive line (nose guard-linebacker-tackle). Tell the players to move at full speed, but not full contact, and use dummy pads. Before each play, have the offense call the play, in effect naming the hole the ball will go through (no ball carrier is needed). The defense tries to penetrate a few feet, and the offense blocks as if a ball carrier is heading through a hole. The defense can call a stunt, or elect to make a head-on attack. The idea is to get the linemen thinking about how to react to the stunt in various situations.

Ends must divide their time between pass-catching fundamentals and blocking (mainly blocking in youth ball). They work out with the linemen against the dummies or the sled for blocking form. They also work with the running backs (and defensive backs) on passing drills.

Ends are called upon to take on defensive linemen head-to-head, and thus must work with other linemen on the blocking charge and jolt. However, they are more often used to make an open-field block on a linebacker or defensive back, so they need to work on specialty blocks such as slant and downfield blocks. They also cross block with the tackle. Downfield blocking is tough to do well, usually because it is not practiced enough. A good drill, called *5 blocker,* is to have three ends practice against each other. Line two of them up about 5 yards apart, with a third end in the middle. Put cones about 5 yards to either side. One end must try to tag the other end, who tries to run by him while the one in the middle tries to block. Stop the play a few seconds after contact is made.

The other half of "fundamentals time" for ends is spent on running pass patterns. An end should work on controlling the defender. The best way, as stated in chapter three, is to run right at the defender and cut just as the defender changes his motion or balance. The end also needs to try body fakes to get a defender leaning the wrong way. And, last but not least, he must concentrate on the ball in flight and on receiving the ball. Part of his time should be spent catching passes using down-and-in, down-and-out, and deep patterns. He should be encouraged to pretend there is a defender on him and go through fakes and sharp cuts. The remainder of his time is spent with defensive backs who try to break up the play. (Tell players not to tackle, but to go for the ball only.) Coaches should run actual pass plays without letting the defenders know what the pattern is. It is essential to teach receivers to "see" the whole field, look for gaps, and know where the defenders are.

Sometimes an end or wide receiver faces close coverage trying to stall him at the line, which can be done legally in the first 5 yards from scrimmage. Try to simulate this at practice. The end should attack the defender, and then give him a head and shoulder fake without letting the defender get his hands into the end's body. Tell the receiver to push down on the defender's hands with one arm and use the other to swing free.

The goal for every receiver is to catch a great number of passes. As in all sports, repetition leads to perfection. Use two or three quarterbacks, or use coaches if your quarterbacks aren't accurate yet, to throw to multiple lines of defenders: one line left, one right, and one deep. At one point, tell everyone to try to catch short passes with one hand. Rotate quarterbacks. One good drill is to place a receiver in a semicircle of four other receivers, with two footballs. He throws the first ball to one of the players in the semicircle and another throws the second ball to him. He has to react quickly to be able to pass and catch both balls. After a while, another receiver goes to the middle.

Running backs need to spend a lot of time with the quarterback practicing running patterns. They must perfect the handoff and work on timing as various running backs cross in front of each other or lead the ball carrier. The first team should practice together. Coaches should focus on form and the other fundamentals listed in chapter three. Have your checklist handy and focus on each point. Look at the mechanics of the handoff: the position of outer and inner arms, the hands curled around the tips of the ball, the ball carried away from the nearest tackler. (See figure 7-5 on page 135.)

Running backs need to work with the ends on pass patterns and on pass-receiving fundamentals. They also need to work on blocking. Chapter three addressed open field blocking. A good drill for backs is the *5 blocker* drill mentioned previously for ends.

Running backs must protect the ball. At all levels of football, turnovers decide the game. Some time *must* be spent every week on ball security. A good drill is to have the quarterback simulate a snap and then hand off to a running back. A few yards away, position two players (two other running backs) with dummy pads. Their job is to jolt the running back with the pads just after he gets the ball and to use a free hand to strip the ball. The runner must go between the two players. This can also be done with a gauntlet of players with dummies, all trying to slow the runner and strip the ball. Another drill is to have four players surround the back (who does not try to run) and try to strip the ball from him in four to five seconds.

Backs should also practice switching the ball from one arm to the other to move it away from the nearest tackler. A good drill is the *slalom*: Line up six or more backs in a zigzag pattern. A back with the ball slaloms past this line, switching the ball from arm to arm as he approaches each player (he should nudge each player). The defending players take a swipe at the ball (not the runner). Then the runner takes his position at the end of the pattern and the first back in the pattern takes a shot at the slalom. Run it until each player gets several turns.

Quarterbacks and **centers** should take a dozen snaps a day in addition to the snaps during drills. They can't get enough of this routine, and anyone experienced with youth football knows how often the ball is lost on bad snaps. The players may get bored with it, but it must be practiced. Line up a dummy opposite the center and give the center a jolt with the pad upon the snap. Always have the quarterback drop back

7-5. **HANDOFFS**

Practice handoff mechanics. It is boring, but essential, to work on timing for running plays.

or pivot when practicing snaps since it makes no sense to practice a stationary snap becaue it will never occur in a game. A good diagnostic drill is to have the quarterback take snaps with only his top hand. If the ball falls straight down without turning or spinning, the snap is good. Quarterbacks should be encouraged to spend a lot of time fooling with the ball.

Of course, as noted earlier for ends and running backs, the quarterback must spend time practicing passing patterns, working on the timing of passes with the moves made by receivers, and also practicing handoffs and pitch-outs to his running backs. A quarterback should always have a ball in his hands—spinning it up into the air, droppint it and catching it with one hand, juggling it, exchanging it behind the back and between the legs. I remember Phil Simms, formerly of the Giants, doing this constantly on the sidelines. Quarterbacks should squeeze tennis balls and perform other exercises to strengthen their wrists. They should practice passing while on the run, while jumping, while on one knee, and even while on their backs. Quarterbacks should practice a three-, five-, and seven-step drop, always retreating quickly, as well as throwing with the nose of the ball up (for long passes) and with it even or down a bit (for short passes). Check their grip of the ball, and adjust it if needed.

The **punter** and the **field-goal kicker** must work with the center on long snaps. Your starting punt and kickoff receiver needs to practice receptions. Have the three of them practice repetitions once or twice a week. Remember the fundamentals, and keep your checklist handy. Don't take specialty teamwork for granted, as this is often where mistakes are made. Kickoffs, punts, and field goals all need to be practiced at least once a week. The day before a game is the best time to practice.

4. Work on team execution of plays—sixty minutes per practice. Individual skills and proper form must come together on the field. The offense must spend a considerable portion of practice time on running plays. Live, contact scrimmage is of course the most effective way to accomplish this, but it is also a good way to increase injuries. I don't recommend a full scrimmage more than once a week. Never allow tackling of the quarterback on pass plays; two-hand touch is the limit.

You can conduct scrimmages by running plays against a defense with dummy pads. Your scouting reports should tell you which defensive and offensive formations the other team will run on game day, and you need to practice your own strategies against these systems. Have the players run at half speed and freeze when they make contact. Then you can discuss what they did or should have done. Check to ensure the shoulder and head are playside. On passing plays, tell the pass defense to drop the pads and play for the ball only. Run each play until everyone gets it right. Use defensive stunts to make it difficult and realistic for the offense.

Live scrimmages are usually held midweek to give players a day or two to get over any soreness before the weekend game. Keep your eye on the matchups so no one is seriously overmatched and gets repeatedly belted. The players are well padded, but make sure you reduce the possibility of injury, particularly at grade-school levels. Use a quick whistle. Blow plays dead if a runner gets into the secondary to reduce open field tackling. I recommend players move only at three-quarter speed. Early on, you may want to go full speed here and there to find out who your real tigers are. Practice is about form and execution more than blood and guts.

THE PRACTICE PLAN

Each practice should have a written practice plan. You can double the value of each practice if you are well organized.

Your practice plans should vary over the course of the season. The first weeks of practice in the fall season are for conditioning, deciding what positions should be assigned to each player, teaching proper form, and executing running plays. After a few weeks and as games approach, shift the focus to individual skills, special teams, and then to team dynamics. *All of these elements, however, should be a part of the plan at every practice all year.*

One more thing to remember: Always keep practices humming. Watch the pace carefully to make sure things are moving. During team drills, especially running plays, keep the plays rolling. Of course, you need to comment on form and correct execution, but keep it moving. You need repetition, and you can get many more plays in by cutting out unnecessary activity. You don't always need huddles, and plays can be called from ready positions.

PRACTICE PLAN

5:55 P.M. Early birds do *Quick Cali Set*, run a warm-up lap.

6:00 P.M. Conditioning: Team lines up in rows. Do three to four stretches from the Stretch Set.
Speed Drills: Robot, Bounce, Buttkick, Goosestep. (Do 2.)
Agility Drills: Simon Says, Carioca, Rope Drill. (Do 1-2.)
Entire team runs one lap around the field.

6:25 P.M. Call team together for comments.

6:30 P.M. Fundamentals: Two groups: linemen and backs

Linemen and Ends: Down-Set-Hut or Dummy Drill (fifteen minutes). Finish with Unirail drill.

Backs: 1) Review running back form for stance, pivot, and first step; have the quarterback and center practice hikes and practice legwork for drop steps. (fifteen minutes). 2) Practice handoff mechanics between quarterback and running backs.

Punter and place-kicker: Work fifteen minutes on kicks at other end of field. Punt receiver catches.

Or:

Linemen: Practice defensive shiver against dummy pads (fifteen minutes). Finish with Bull in the Middle Drill

Backs and Ends: Pass practice lines, use the entire passing tree (fifteen minutes). Run play patterns.

Or:

Linemen: 1) Do Timing Drill for defensive charge on center snap (fifteen minutes). 2) Practice charge, jolt, and drive on sled.

Backs and Ends: 1) Ball security drills using players with dummy pads or shields who swipe at the ball. 2) Practice running patterns.

Or:

Linemen: Hold 'em Drill (fifteen minutes). Pick a Lane Drill.

Backs and Ends: Practice downfield blocking on dummy pads.

6:55 P.M. Water break.

7:00 P.M. Team Practice: Run offensive plays against defense; defensemen have dummy pads (thrity minutes). Practice kickoffs, punts, place kicks, kickoff returns, punt returns, points after touchdowns. (Pick one specialty per day. No tackling. Half-speed contact on blocking or use dummy pads.)

Or:

Team Practice: Offensive scrimmage (thrity minutes). Defensive scrimmage (twenty-five minutes).

7:55 P.M. Wind Sprints: Line up by position: linemen, ends, backs.

8:00 P.M. Closing Comments; practice over.

GAME DAY

Of course, the entire practice week is in preparation for game day. The game is what it's all about. However, there are several things you need to do specifically for the game. Certain parents should have the responsibility for water and oranges. An assistant coach or captain leads stretching exercises. Practice of punts, punt receptions, and place kicks should be handled by the special teams coach. Quarterbacks and receivers should take ten minutes for a passing drill after warm-ups.

FIVE KEYS TO GAME DAY PREPARATION

1. The game plan. Usually, experienced coaches know, or some other coach in the league will know, what types of offenses and defenses opponents employ. If not, get a parent to scout a practice or a game. Your scouting report will tell you the types of plays the opponent will run, the types of defenses they use and in what situations, how they stunt, what their strengths and weaknesses are, and how good their special teams are. Early in the week, meet with your coaches and develop your game plan using this information. Create a list of plays you will use and the situations you will use them in (second and long, third and short, and so forth). You will have already gotten a sense of your "go-to" plays from prior games or scrimmages. Practice them until the team knows them cold and practice against the defenses you expect to see. Your game plan is a sheet of plays sorted by the situations where you will use them.

2. Depth chart. List your first, second, and third teams, both offense and defense. Most coaches use colors or terms to designate the teams. Also list your specialty teams. The depth cart is listed by position, with the second and third teamers next to each other, so you can quickly substitute names in the event of an injury. An assistant coach is in charge of these lists and is responsible for keeping kids, especially substitutes aware of which teams they are on.

3. Playing time. A coach or a team parent keeps a list of all kids and how many plays they participate in. The rules will require eight to twelve plays each, and you need to know by the end of the third quarter who is short and by how many plays. Usually, a team will substitute the second string offense for a full series of downs, or even a full possession. It's better to get subs their mandatory playing time on offense, since a second team defense can quickly give up points. Another good time to sub is when a player underperforms in his effort—dogging it, not hustling—and it's a good time to give another player a chance to show what he's got. (See the glossary for more information on substitution rules.)

139

4. Evaluation of the opposition. Every coach needs to know what the other team is doing. All coaches should keep notes: How is the opponent deviating from the scouting report? What adjustments need to be made? Are there mismatches on the line or in the defense? Is anyone on your team hurt? What plays are working? Listen to your players; they will often know who they can beat. At halftime, discuss these notes and revise the game plan as needed.

5. Special notes. Have a coach or parent record special moments, big plays, penalties committed, errors—anything that you will want to address at practice the next week. Try to let players know at once, but make sure it's listed so you can come back to it.

THE PSYCHOLOGY OF COACHING FOOTBALL

08

ON THE IMPORTANCE OF WINNING

*Our society is ferociously competitive in spirit. Pressuring children
too hard may turn them into adults so obsessed with being
first that they get no joy out of life except in the narrow field of
competition. They never give nor get pleasure in their relationships
with spouses, children, friends, and fellow workers.*

—Dr. Benjamin Spock

Winning isn't everything; it's the only thing!

—Coach Vince Lombardi

It's hard to imagine two more opposite views, and from two such well-regarded people. They capture the essence of a controversy that rages on in our youth programs, schools, and even our government. Are winning and competition necessary experiences for young people as they prepare to enter the business world? Or are they a distraction from learning to do one's best, for its own sake, and an unfortunate source of stress and malady among our youth?

Well, it's impossible to deal squarely with this issue. However, what is clear to me after a lifetime of playing and coaching youth sports is that the coach is the key to how these issues affect the kids on the team. At the heart of how good a coach you will be is how well you balance your need to win with your responsibility to develop healthy young people. This balance affects your every action, your relationship with each player, and the atmosphere on the field. It will characterize the memories of your coaching experience for many, many years to come. In striking that balance, you will engage in a continuing struggle with the passions of competition.

141

The point is that *it is a balance*. Dr. Spock and Coach Lombardi had points of view grounded in their own experiences. For instance, we all worry a bit about the total dedication required of young Olympic athletes, having sacrificed much of their youth for their quests. Yet, we know they have enjoyed moments of glory that seem to transcend life itself, achieving heights most of us only dream about.

It's not realistic, and therefore not helpful, to have experts tell us that analysis of years of psychological research proves that competition is poison. That's like telling us not to breathe because the air is somewhat polluted! Let's face it—we all know kids who could excel, but do not. They just need a push to get going.

By the same token, many of us will remember the ugly scene on national television when competitive fires drove Ohio State coaching legend Woody Hayes to attack an opposing Clemson player on the field. And we cringed when young teen star Mary Pierce, symbolic of many troubled young athletes, had to obtain a restraining order against her father for pressuring her. We're all too familiar with unbridled frenzy to win, often riding on the dark horse of fear of failure.

This issue goes to the essence of the human condition. It is part of our evolution. The answers are complex and most elusive. I know that some schools have abandoned competitive interaction in their physical education programs to avoid damaging the feelings of kids who are not outstanding. Isn't it better that kids learn about and prepare for the experience of success and failure in a controlled setting inside the relatively harmless gymnasium than in the crucible of adult life? We shouldn't abandon the struggle to succeed just because we haven't figured out how, as a society, to do it right. We couldn't quit if we wanted to. It's part of life, and we need to continue to work to find the right balance.

I think if we locked Coach Lombardi and Dr. Spock in the same room they would probably find common ground. Lombardi knew better than most coaches that the key to success in football is in knowing how to motivate athletes to win the personal struggle to do your best, to improve beyond your limits, spurred on by your team's goals. He said that the spirit, the will to win, the will to excel—these are the important things that transcend the game itself.

Joe Paterno, the legend-in-his-own-time coach of Penn State, talked about winning in his book *Football My Way* (MacMillan, 1971):

Nothing in life, including football, is worthwhile unless you enjoy it and gain something from the experience. Like a skier going down a mountain, you should be doing it for the sheer enjoyments of it, not because you have to win or are afraid to lose. Sure, we're trying to win football games and we're not going to be satisfied with anything less than a 10-0 record, but I don't want it to ruin our lives if we lose. I don't want Penn State to become the kind of place where an 8-2 season is a tragedy. You can't tell kids that a football loss is a tragedy because it's not. All I ask them to do is to give their best. If we win, Great! If we lose, it's not the end of the world. There is another game Saturday. I don't want my players crying. I want them to feel bad, but not ashamed. I'll never buy that stuff some coaches say that if a boy loses a game he is a loser for life. The coaches with that attitude, that winning is the only thing, don't belong in football.

Tom Landry, the Hall of Fame former Dallas Cowboys coach, agreed in his autobiography, *Tom Landry* (Zondervan, 1990):

If winning is the only thing that matters, then you'd do anything to win. You'd cheat. You'd sacrifice your marriage or your family to win. Relationships wouldn't matter. People wouldn't matter. Winning would be worth any price you had to pay. I don't believe that; after working with Vince Lombardi day after day for six years, I know he didn't believe it either. A more accurate reflection of his feelings would require a revision to that famous quote, to read "Winning isn't everything, it's the effort to win that matters."

However, it's fair to say that Paterno and Landry do not represent the majority of college or NFL coaches, who must produce wins or lose their jobs. This win-at-all-costs attitude filters down through high school and certainly to Pop Warner leagues. I've seen it repeatedly.

How you resolve the balance between winning and individual development is up to you. If you recognize the need to strike a balance, you are off to a good start. My own approach in coaching is probably best characterized as a struggle back and forth around that balance. When I find myself too focused on the win, I step back. Let's be honest—we don't see many perfect models of balance because the emotions and competitive fires that naturally arise on the football field during play can be quite powerful.

I believe most coaches want to build character and provide a positive experience for each player while also trying to win the game. There are some who never really challenge their teams for fear of upsetting the kids, and these "nice guys" don't do much damage. Of course, their players may never rise to the next level of play. Other coaches, at the opposite extreme, feel compelled to win at any cost, and the cost can be tragic for the fragile psyche of a young boy. Find the middle ground.

143

Of course, the issues vary with the age of your team. At preteen football levels, the emphasis should be heavily on developing the individual. This is why most programs require that all kids play a certain amount of time. By the time of high school varsity play, the balance between winning and individual development is more even. It should never get further than that, but the reality of major collegiate play is that losing coaches don't last.

ON MOTIVATION

Rock, I know I'm going to die. I'm not afraid. But someday, Rock, when things on the field are going against us, tell the boys, Rock, to go out there and win just one for the Gipper. Now, I don't know where I'll be then, coach. But I'll know about it, and I'll be happy.

—George Gipp

Legendary Notre Dame coach Knute Rockne waited eight years until, during halftime in a big game against Army, he repeated these last words of his dying quarterback in what was to become the epitome of halftime motivation. It's a beautiful story, but coaches must rely on more than halftime speeches to motivate their teams. Sure, some coaches have that charismatic quality to motivate a team by the sheer strength of their personalities. Rockne and Lombardi are the models of the "hero" coach. However, the rest of us mere "mortal" guys need to consider motivational techniques that can help us get the job done. The secrets to good motivation are easily found in the growing science of sports psychology. Once considered mere gobbledygook, the mental aspect of competition is now a cornerstone of athletic development at the highest levels of amateur and professional sports. Many teams, including the U.S. Olympic program, have employed full-time sports psychologists for many years.

It is not the purpose of this book to go in great depth into the psychology of sports. You will find aspects of psychology spread throughout this book, as well as in my books on coaching other youth sports such as baseball, basketball, and soccer. I have used psychological insight throughout my twenty years of coaching, and you will see that much of this is common sense, obvious to any caring adult. The first chapter of this book focuses directly on the right mental approach to the game. My checklist approach to teaching form is consistent with the mental checklist urged for athletes by sports psychologists. The following are some emerging motivational techniques that seem to work best for youth football.

144

ATTABOY!

There never will be a better tool than frequent positive reinforcement for young athletes in any sport. This is especially true for football. Since the coach so often has the occasion to bellow at players to get them psyched up, it becomes essential to liberally give out some "attaboys" for good effort. In 1983, Dr. Nathan J. Smith, a consultant for the American Board of Pediatrics, studied two groups of coaches. He found that the single most important difference in the research between coaches to whom young athletes relate least favorably was the frequency with which coaches reinforce and reward desirable behavior. A pat on the back, a smile, clapping, praise, a wink and a nod, as well as tangible rewards, such as decals on the helmet or more playing time, all go a very long way toward motivating high performance.

I would add that the rewards are even more effective when they emphasize outstanding effort as opposed to great results. An athlete has complete control over the amount of effort he puts into his game. The results, however, are dependent on a number of things, many of which are beyond the individual's control. Even corrective action, pointing out mistakes, should be sandwiched within some positive comments; for example, "Good try, Jack. Next time, drive the shoulder into the midsection and wrap the arms—you can do it!"

Football coaches spend a lot of time hollering, trying to motivate players, and developing that all-important desire to overcome the opponent. It's a tough sport, and kids shouldn't be holding back. However, there is a line that must not be crossed—and that is the humiliation of a player. The idea is to be firm to let players know that they can do better if they reach deeper into their gut. I like to ask players if they gave it their best shot. "Was that your best effort?" or "Don't you have more 'pop' than that?" Let a player know what you think about his effort, not about him personally. Don't personalize your criticism. A kid can relate to trying harder, but he can't relate positively if you tell him he stinks. Explain the problem with fundamentals or form so that he understands the concept. Be patient until he gets the idea. Be clear in how you communicate to players.

Most important, reward good effort openly and liberally. Praise a good jolt. Recognize hustle. Yell out, "That's football!" It can get infectious, with all players trying to hear the sound of a good pop.

WE ARE FAMILY!

I've read the autobiographies of many great coaches. The one constant theme in all of their stories is the ability to relate closely to the different individuals on their team

145

and to create a family-type environment. Each kid is different, whether on a team or in a family, and each one needs a personal approach. Even the least effective players should be treated with the same respect as the best players. I like to start each season with a group discussion on what it means to be on a team. I would tell the players that for the rest of the season, they are all friends. They are all in a special relationship with each other. I said they should say hello in the school hallways and help each other out both on and off the field. I never tolerate criticism of a teammate on the field, and quickly bench any offender. Kids are expected to urge each other on, to quickly tell a teammate to put a mistake behind him. I promote team dinners and outings and move to break up cliques.

Joe Paterno said in *Football My Way*, "If we could get that feeling—that 'we' and 'us' instead of 'I' and 'me'—so you can feel the love and respect for each other, they lose that individuality for the good of the team. When they lose themselves in something they think is a bit bigger than they are, they will be tough to beat."

Teambuilding is a proven ticket to success. The concept is widely used in all walks of life. But it doesn't just happen because a bunch of kids are on a team. It happens when coaches work at it. Put it in the practice plan, talk to your assistant coaches about it, and then opportunities to promote "teamness" will present themselves in abundance.

ON PEAK PERFORMANCE

The bane of coaches is whatever it is that makes a kid play great one day and fall apart the next. A kid gets knocked on his back during the opening series and winds up getting pushed around all day. Another kid doesn't get blocked, makes a good tackle, and suddenly starts to terrorize the line of scrimmage. One day the halfback can't find the hole even if he could roll through it sideways; other days his cutbacks seem transcendent.

Modern science tells us that how athletes cope with the stress of the challenge before them is all "upstairs," at least much of it. Mental control begins with the commonly known fight-or-flight instinct; that is, the natural impulse that arises in cornered animals to respond to a threat by fighting it or fleeing from it. It is a genetic reaction, inherited in humans from our ancient ancestors. This same reaction, under game conditions, can create a panic that distracts concentration and can even cause muscles to spasm. However, when controlled properly, it can lead the athlete to a zone of peak performance.

In its February 14, 1994, issue, *U.S. News & World Report*, in an article entitled "The Inner Game of Winning," reported on the research of Stanford University neurobiologist

Robert Sapolsky. He found that the properly controlled response to challenge releases a desirable increase in adrenalin and sugar, producing the sense of "heightened awareness and flow" associated with being in a peak "zone." The negative counterpart of this reaction, which he calls the "fearful" response, produces a bodily cocktail laced with a substance called cortisol that can "not only impair performance, but can also lead over the long run to damage of the arteries and liver and lead to depression."

One result emerging from this science is the notion of *tapering*. Tapering is the term used to describe the process of bringing the body to a state where peak performance can occur. At its most basic, tapering is the cutting back of volume, frequency, or duration, thus reducing fatigue and stress. This allows the body to fully recover and rebuild itself.

What does all of this have to do with kids playing football? Well, for one thing, it helps us learn how to minimize that inconsistency we complained about at the beginning of this section. The research tells us what steps can be taken to create the conditions optimal to peak performance. It means that Saturday practice should not be too taxing, and that the week before a big game is time to focus on execution, not conditioning.

Some of this we already do and have done for years. The time-honored way to produce a controlled response to game-day excitement is constant repetition during practice. Much of this book deals with the need to repeatedly go over play patterns, form, and concepts. The responses become automatic and can occur even if the player is under stress or overly excited.

A ritual-like approach to game day is conducive to the relaxed state of mind needed. A regular pattern of eating, exercise, dressing, and pre-game discussion is highly recommended. Try to avoid any surprises or deviations. The preset mental routine should apply right up to the snap of the ball during the game. Players should be encouraged to run through a checklist of form (e.g., head up, prepare to jolt, drive the forearm into the midsection). Tell them to mentally picture the play, imagining themselves with great form jolting the opponent, dashing through a hole, or eluding the grasp of a tackler. They should do this right up to the hike of the ball. It works. It is well accepted at the highest levels of sport. Tell kids that they need to prepare the mind as well as the body if they are to reach their potential.

Sapolsky notes that premature arousal of adrenalin hours before the game can result in the level in the blood dropping after a few hours, even to a point below normal at game time. This will lead to sub-par performance and is another reason to have relaxed and stable pre-game routines. Certainly don't let the team scream and holler in the bus all the way to the game. Some coaches employ Zen-type meditations in their training programs, providing athletes with methods to cause relaxed states of mind at will.

Sports psychologists have anticipated this research in their support for mental imaging of athletic routines. Olympic athletes have been imaging their steps mentally for years. What we have now are clear scientific bases for these approaches. These techniques are useful at all levels of play. They are perhaps most needed at the youngest levels, where kids have less ability to control the anxieties of competition. Relaxed game day rituals, mental imaging, affirmations for self-esteem, mental checklists such as those contained throughout this book (for example, a defender must charge, neutralize, shed, focus, drive, and wrap a ball carrier) are techniques that can be repeatedly practiced.

GET AN EDGE

Many coaches have some concept that they repeatedly use to focus players on achieving peak performance. I always told my players to try to *get an edge* over their opponent. We talked about how competitors are usually physically similar, and so the winner would be the one who has some kind of edge over his opponent. This concept helped me to get kids to accept, for instance, the idea of improving their mental approach—as one way to get an edge. I would tell kids to double the number of push-ups they could do, since kids on other teams probably weren't doing it.

Don Shula is the winningest NFL coach of all time. He used the concept to its fullest and named his autobiography, *The Winning Edge* (E.P. Dutton & Co., 1974). He said in the book, "It is my firm belief that the concept of The Winning Edge and our ability to drive it home to the players helped produce the perfect season we [the Miami Dolphins] experienced in 1972." Need I say more?

HOW DO YOU WANT TO BE REMEMBERED?

In the final analysis, youth football is about boys becoming men. You need to know that most boys join the team for reasons very different from what you would hope for. Many of them believe that football players are the in-crowd, or that football players get the attention of the girls. Others are looking to build themselves up physically, get in shape, or find a way to release pent-up frustration. Some do it just because friends do it, and they are seeking camaraderie. Others do it because Dad told them they had to.

Most Pop Warner-level players won't play on varsity at the high-school level, and only a few of them may play in college. You will probably never coach a future professional football player. It is doubtful that they will remember much about last season

148

twenty years from now, and certainly not the scores of various games. But I guarantee you one thing. They will remember *you* for the rest of their lives. The memories of my coaches are etched clearly on my mind. I remember them vividly, for good or for bad. You will not remember all of the kids you coached, particularly if you do it for a number of years, but every one of them will remember you. How do you want to be remembered?

The relationship between a coach and a player is a powerful one. You are a not only a father figure (most football coaches are men), but you are the ultimate authority for what is, in a kid's mind, the most important thing in all of life. Through his football experience, he is learning important things about himself, and he will always associate this experience with you. I always viewed coaching as an awesome responsibility. You may want to ignore the larger picture, but sticking your head in the sand does not change what is really going on. There are many tools you can use to help you make the experience a good one, whether your team wins or loses. But in the final analysis it comes down to whether you can accept the larger role of being both a coach and a friend.

Vince Lombardi, who coached St. Cecilia's High School in New Jersey at one point, spoke of the role of a coach in an interview recorded in *The Vince Lombardi Scrapbook* (Grosset & Dunlap, 1976). Speaking about high school coaches, he said:

Well, he's probably the only man in the whole school who can do anything about discipline. And to do that, the first thing I would tell that coach is to be himself. The number one objective you must have is to sell yourself to them, honestly, from the heart. What you are teaching has to be what you are.

Joe Paterno added:

First of all, a coach has to be a teacher ... not just of skills but of character qualities and some values in life.... He has to be a leader ... to make the players identify with him, and to develop morale.... He must be able to develop three things in an athlete: pride, poise, and self-confidence.

It's much more than just Xs and Os.

PARENTS AND COACHES

Football games are loud places. The game seems to fire up everyone, and so you will have to go with the flow. The noise is part of it all. Unfortunately, there are always a few super screamers—parents who get out of control. They look quite foolish and are very irritating to sit near. It is as if they have been given a license to leave their senses. Sure, everyone cheers loudly on a big play, but don't be a spectacle. Have some consideration for the fans around you.

Most important, be positive. Don't unduly criticize everyone, especially your own child. If you criticize another player, chances are his parents are nearby. What purpose does this type of outburst serve? Don't take out your frustrations on a kid when he makes a mistake. It embarrasses both of you, and it only teaches the child to play less confidently. I guarantee that all kids will make mistakes and they will not improve if you punctuate the game with "What's the matter with you?" or "That was stupid!" or "If you don't get going, I'll...." That kind of talk is disastrous.

If you cannot control yourself, then stay home. This may sound tough, but you will do a lot of damage to your child and to your relationship with your child if you don't control your anger. Some people just can't keep it in, so avoid damage by staying home. I've seen this problem often, and it really can screw a kid up. If you must yell, then say things like "Tough D," "Stay low," or "Let's go." Congratulate a good effort. Let the coach call the plays.

Interfering parents are a major problem for coaches in most sports. It seems less so in football than in some other sports, and that may be because parents are usually sitting farther away from the team. In baseball, they are right on top of the team, and their complaining seems more visible. Nonetheless, it is a problem in all sports.

I have no problem with the parent who is just trying to communicate with the coach and find out whether there is an issue they need to be aware of. But often, they are argumentative and downright insulting.

Of course, coaches don't need to take any abuse from a pain in the neck parent. But before you get too defensive, think about what's going on. Most parents feel helpless when they see their son going through a bad time. Maybe he is not playing much and is having self-doubts. He may be acting up at home or school because of it. Parents feel the pain along with their kids, so hear them out. Help them to understand the problem, and perhaps focus on things they can do to help their son. If their problem is how they feel you are treating their child, tell them that you are "on" him because you think he can do better and that you are trying to arouse his potential. Maybe you can get some insight into what is troubling a young man or what is holding him back.

Most of all, keep in mind that *he's their kid!* They may feel a bit threatened by your control over their child. As a parent myself, I have had a few uneasy feelings about coaches. It's quite natural. A little patience on your part can defuse some strong emotions. You can turn a potential feud into something that helps the boy, and ultimately the team.

HOW TO TREAT THE COACH

I hope you read this book and practice with your child for a while before you ever meet your child's first football coach. Then you can offer your help as an assistant. The best way to deal with the coach is to join with him. By the way, when kids are only seven to eight years old, there is not much skill on the field to worry about. It is a good starting place for inexperienced coaches.

If you don't coach, I suggest you find another way to get involved. When the coach calls, offer whatever help you can give. If your job prohibits helping on weekdays, offer to help on weekends. Many coaches will be happy for it. They need people to do stats at games, keep the footballs clean and dry, run the first-down chains, organize the water trays, and many other things. If you run into a coach who doesn't want help, there's not much you can do officially, but you can still work with your child at home.

Just call, e-mail, or walk up to the coach at the first practice and ask if you can help. Some parents like to sit and watch practice. I don't mind, and most coaches won't, either. It will help you become aware of areas where your child can use some improvement.

If your child is playing the minimum amount of time, but only the minimum, be fair before you approach the coach. Usually, coaches are out to win, and therefore they use the best players. Tell your child to work harder, and he may improve enough to play more. If the coach is being unfair, talk to him about it. It is a difficult thing for all involved, so please be sure it's not just your ego complaining. And, for goodness sake, keep your child out of the debate. Kids don't need the negative images involved. Don't get mad—but don't avoid confrontation, either. A few questions to the coach, nicely stated, will help.

First of all, the coach is giving up a lot of time to coach the team and deserves a lot of room. If you want to coach, sign up to do so or to help. Show up at practices or at club meetings to offer help. That earns you the right to give your opinion. Otherwise, be very conservative about offering it.

Second, realize your bias. You are a parent and you love your son. You may think that he deserves to play more or to play another position, but the coach knows a lot more about what all the kids can do and who has earned playing time. It's unfair to ask for more time for your kid, and unfair to the other kids to suggest that one of them should play less. Just work more with your child so he improves, and he will play more. Coaches want to win, and they usually give the better players more playing time.

However, coaches need to learn, too. And sometimes they are going about things quite wrong. If this is the case, then gently indicate how you feel. It is important that you think about it a lot and make sure you know what you are talking about before you say anything. Question your own bias. If you still feel you can help, offer your opinion. Avoid an argument, or even a long debate. Make your point and ask the coach to think about it. Indicate that you are only trying to help. I strongly suggest not being argumentative. Say your piece, listen to the coach, thank him for his time, and end it. If you are lucky, the coach will be thankful. However, he may resent your interference and possibly even take it out on your child. If the situation becomes very bad, let your club president or school athletic director know how you feel. Keep in mind that if your child gets in the middle, he may suffer for it. If the experience is more damaging than good, remove your child from the team.

But remember: think about it, get advice, talk to other parents, and avoid being unduly disruptive. The point of football is to have fun—both watching and playing.

BOYS AND GIRLS

Girls play football and can be very competitive. Any athlete who can perform has a clear right to do so, and this right is protected under federal law in most states. At very young ages, girls and boys are close in speed and aggressiveness and much closer in strength than in later years. At this level, girls can clearly play the game. But they rarely do, and perhaps this is in recognition that there is little future for them in the game. All-girl teams in high school are unheard of. Also, as I noted earlier, football is less about the precision skills that girls can achieve and more about sheer strength, which does not come as easily to most girls, though some can achieve it.

A young girl should never be denied the chance to try it. If she is gifted and determined, particularly at a young age, why not? I admire the girls who have done it under great media pressure, and perhaps someday it will grow as a women's sport.

About one hundred girls play high-school football each year across the country. The pioneers of women's football have set the precedent and paved the way. It may be that the media and critics of women in football have focused too much on players, such as Tawana Hammonds, a female high school player in Maryland whose internal injuries cost her a spleen and half her pancreas. She sued her school's board of education for not properly informing her of the inherent risks of playing football. But this scenario should not diminish the accomplishment of the many hundreds of others who had a great experience with the game, players like Sally Phillips of Spanish River, Florida, a place-kicker who was crowned homecoming queen while wearing full football gear because she had no time to dress after practice. Split end Sarah Price of Chamblee, Georgia, had the most uncommon experience of playing head-to-head against cornerback April Smith of Seneca, South Carolina. In 1985, Carol White became the nation's first collegiate female football coach at Georgia Tech, working with punters and place-kickers.

Professional women's football has had fits and starts since 1926, when the Frankfort Yellow Jackets employed a women's team as halftime entertainment. Since 2000, however, the sport has started to flourish. The National Women's Football Association (NWFA) was formed in 2000 and grew steadily to over forty teams by 2006. There are several other leagues, including the Women's Professional Football League, which started in 1965, and the Independent Women's Football League.

If a girl wants to play the game, she should start at the grade-school level. The competition will be more even, and she will have a chance to see what potential is there. As a coach, you must treat her the same as any other player on the team.

08

09

You can do only so much to improve athletic ability, but you can do a great deal to maintain good heath. Football is a rugged contact sport, and a healthy body goes a long way toward better performance on the field and avoiding injury.

DIET

Obviously, a balanced diet is essential. There are many books on diet, and your doctor, school nurse, or team trainer can also advise you. Good nutrition helps develop strength, endurance, and concentration. A good diet balances proteins, carbohydrates, and fats. An athlete in training needs mainly complex carbohydrates, at least 70 percent of the total diet, with fats (10 percent) and proteins (20 percent) splitting the remainder. A popular useful guide is the food guide pyramid. Complex carbohydrates dominate the base grouping, calling for greater doses of breads, cereal, rice, and pasta. Vegetables and fruits respectively take up the next level, calling for a few daily servings each. The dairy group and the meat, fish, and poultry group are next, with fats last.

Early in the season, particularly during double sessions in the heat at the end of the summer, a dinner high in carbohydrates helps maintain energy for the next day. Pasta is the best meal for this. A banana each day during this intensive period helps prevent potassium depletion. Complex carbohydrates are the primary source of fuel and energy for the athlete. They are broken down into glucose, the body's main source of energy. What is not needed is stored for future use. Avoid simple carbohydrates such as sugar and honey. The old adage that a candy bar just before a game gives an energy boost is misleading since simple carbohydrates cause unstable supplies of glucose (ever notice how tired you feel after a sweets overload?). Good sources of complex carbohydrates are corn on the cob, wild rice, brown rice, whole wheat, and whole rye.

A TYPICAL HIGH-CARBOHYDRATE DIET
Breakfast

- 8 ounces orange juice or a grapefruit or 8 ounces apple juice
- Bowl of shredded wheat (low-fat milk) or oatmeal or cream of farina
- (a) Bacon and two eggs or (b) pancakes and butter
- Several slices of whole-wheat toast and butter
- Daily vitamin
- 10 ounces water

Lunch

- 1 bowl of soup: chicken, clam chowder, or vegetable
- 2 pieces broiled chicken or 6 ounces broiled fish
- Green salad with oil and vinegar
- Cooked rice or a potato (no french fries)
- 2 slices of enriched bread
- 12 to 16 ounces milk
- 10 ounces water

Dinner

- 1 bowl of soup: cream of mushroom, cream of potato, or vegetable
- Linguine with tomato or clam sauce
- Baked potato
- Cooked vegetables: corn, broccoli, peas, or beans
- Beverage of choice
- 10 ounces water

Desserts or Snacks

- Bananas, apples, raisins, strawberries, melons
- 10 ounces water

WATER

All teams should allow water breaks, so make sure each player has a water bottle. Mid-practice is not a good time to load up on water, so tell players to limit themselves to a cup at each break. Kids need a couple of quarts a day or more if it's hot outside early in the season. It's a good habit to drink water, so be sure your child has some at each meal. It is also important to drink plenty of fluids before, during, and after practices. Dehydration reduces performance and can lead to serious medical problems.

SLEEP

Sufficient sleep is also a concern. A player starts the season with double sessions of practice, so you won't have to worry too much at first, since he will come right home and hit the pillow. But if he tries to burn the candle at both ends, remind him of the consequences. I find that kids relate better when they consider practical consequences of their actions. Lack of sufficient rest diminishes performance. Diminished performance costs him playing time.

CONDITIONING, STRENGTH TRAINING, AND WEIGHTS

Kids should be encouraged to do some conditioning in the off-season. Until high-school varsity level play, a good program of calisthenics is adequate. Football requires more strength than most sports. It is not, however, an endurance sport, and kids can always find a moment to take a breather. Most coaches concentrate on improving strength and toughness. Of course, jogging won't hurt conditioning, but it may take away needed body weight. Wind sprints are much better, and it never hurts to add them to training sessions.

I will get into weight training on pages 157–159, but I don't encourage it for grade-school players. A calisthenics program that works on legs and the upper body is adequate. Good exercises include the following:

1. Push-ups. Push-ups are a great exercise since upper-body strength is so important to football, and they can be done anytime, anywhere. A player should do fifty to one hundred per day. During games, he will spend most of his time shoving another kid around, and the one with the strongest chest and shoulders will prevail. The upper body gets a better workout if the hands are elevated 6 inches, on some books or a block, so the chest can descend a few inches lower than the hands.

2. Pull-ups. Pull-ups (on an overhead bar) are also quite helpful. These are chin-ups with the hands reversed and spread as wide as possible. Again, upper-body strength is crucial and any help that you can give here will be immediately and quite noticeably rewarded on the field. If you don't have a pull-up bar, upper-body strength can be easily improved with a set of chest expanders, with springs attached to handles. My son would keep them by the television and use them while watching cartoons.

3. Crunches. Partial sit-ups are great for strengthening the midsection. Lie on the back, knees bent, and lift the shoulder blades off the floor.

4. Dips. Dips are popular and great for the upper body. They require parallel bars. With one hand on each bar, the player dips his body so the arms are bent at least 90 degrees, then pushes up, straightening the arms. A single bar can be used for back dips, with the bar held behind the back, dipping to 90 degrees and pushing back up.

5. Rows. Rowing exercises are very good for increasing strength and stamina if you have access to a rowing machine.

6. Squats. Next, and perhaps most important in football, come the legs. Partial squats, bending the knee halfway with some extra weight added, are quite good. Don't bend all the way. Make sure kids are supervised for this.

7. Stadium stairs. The longstanding tradition of running up stairs is excellent.

8. Lunges. A good leg strengthener is the lunge. Step forward and dip until the back leg bends to a 90-degree angle, then push away from the floor and straighten the legs.

9. Neck bridges. Gentle neck exercises are also helpful, since the neck takes a pounding. Neck bridges are probably the best, but be careful not to overdo it. Perhaps you can get a few pillows under the back to reduce the strain initially.

Remember that muscles are like bubble gum. If you stretch gum quickly, it tears or snaps, but if you stretch it slowly, it expands nicely. Stretching before training, practices, or games helps prevent muscles from tearing or snapping. No practice of any kind should begin without slow jogging, jumping jacks (for the ankles), and some general stretching (for the upper thigh, trunk, and neck). Running sideways and backward or any agility exercises are quite good also. See the exercises recommended for practices in the previous chapter.

WEIGHT TRAINING

When I wrote the first edition of this book, I was clear that weight training should be avoided by grade-school level players and not started until mid-high-school years. Part of the reason was intuitive: A child's body is growing rapidly until then. I was also aware of studies done in the 1970s that showed that grade-school kids do not gain much strength from weight lifting due to low levels of male hormones. These studies suggested that there was significant risk of injury to the kid's growth plates, which are the ends of the long bones that account for growth.

A careful study of 354 high school-football players, reported in 1990 by Dr. William Risser of the University of Texas Medical School, found that weight lifting can cause severe musculoskeletal injuries, usually muscle strains often found in the lower back. In the study, 7.1 percent of the players reported injury. Injuries occurred when free weights were used in major lifts, such as the clean and jerk, the snatch, the squat lift, the dead lift, the power clean, and bench, incline, and overhead presses. Injury often occurred in the home and was related to poor technique and form, lack of warm-up, and lack of a spotter to assist.

I'm still against kids lifting weights, but I must report that more recent research suggests a different point of view, at least for high-school kids. In the November 1990 issue of *Pediatrics* (Vol. 86, No. 5), the American Academy of Pediatrics Committee on Sports Medicine stated that "Recent research has shown that short-term programs in which prepubescent [grade-school] athletes are trained and supervised by knowledgeable adults can increase strength without significant injury risk." The statement went on to say:

> *Interscholastic athletic programs in secondary schools are increasingly emphasizing strength training as a conditioning method for participants in male and female sports. The major lifts are often used ... Strength training in adolescence occasionally produces significant musculoskeletal injury ... especially during use of the major lifts. Safety requires careful planning of several aspects of a program. This includes devising a program for the intensity, duration, frequency, and rate of progression of weight use, as well as selection of sport-specific exercises appropriate for the physical maturity of the individual. Proper supervision should be provided during training sessions.*

The committee also addressed the issue of when kids should be allowed to lift maximal amounts of weight, that is, the greatest amount of weight they can successfully lift. They concluded this should be avoided until they have passed their period of maximal velocity of height growth. Young people reach that stage on average at age fifteen; however, the committee also notes that there is "much individual variation." Consequently, based on the contents of this article, the American Academy of Pediatrics recommended that each child's stage of physical maturity be assessed by medical personnel and that the adults planning strength-training programs be qualified to develop programs appropriate for varying stages of maturity.

Another excellent article, "Strength Training in Children and Adolescents" (*Pediatric Clinics of North America*, October 1990), was written by Dr. David Webb at the Center for Sports Medicine at Saint Francis Memorial Hospital in San Francisco, California. He found that most injuries occurred in the home while the child was unsupervised, and that there is not an inordinate risk of injury in weight training if it's properly done. He also reported that strength training can help kids excel in sports, and that it can actually reduce the incidence of muscle or tendon injuries.

A February 2, 2006, note from the Mayo Clinic on their Web site, www.mayo-clinic.com, stated: "Strength training for kids has gotten a bad reputation over the years. Lifting weights, for example, was once thought to damage young growth plates—areas of cartilage that have not yet turned to bone. Experts now realize that with good technique and the right amount of resistance, young athletes can avoid growth plate injuries. Strengthening exercises, with proper training and supervision, provide many benefits to a young athlete."

What does this all mean? Knowledgeable trainers, whether at a private club or hired by the team, can help a player gain strength at any level of play, and strength helps young football players overcome their opponents. Since many kids do it, those who don't will be at a disadvantage. However, any program should avoid maximal weight lifts until the mid-high-school years. Be careful; injury can still occur no matter what.

Let's face it, anyone who has ever lifted weights knows that even if you follow a good program, kids will have a powerful urge to finish with some heavy weights to see how much they can lift. If unsupervised, they will go for the max at some point. This is one of the main reasons I frown on the idea. I also resent the idea that we should heighten the competitive pressure of athletes in grade school by creating a need to strength train in order to "keep up." But the reality is that at the high-school level players need to do weights if they are to be competitive. As a parent, you must ensure that they are supervised and that they follow a sound program. A 7 percent injury rate is quite high, so parents must assert controls on this matter.

If a player undertakes a weight-training program, he should have the supervision and advice of a knowledgeable trainer. Parents should ask their doctor if their son has any preexisting health conditions that can be aggravated by such training. High blood pressure is one condition that doesn't mix with weights. Any pain should be reported to the trainer. Warm-up and stretching exercises should be done before lifting. Lifting maximal weights or engaging in sudden jerking exercises, such as the clean and jerk should not be done. Kids should generally use weights that can be done in sets of fifteen repetitions. They should not lift every day, but every other day at the most. All major muscle groups should get some attention to keep development balanced, although the emphasis in football for weight training is usually on the legs.

09

PLYOMETRICS

Plyometrics is a method of developing power by rapidly stretching and contracting specific muscles under significant resistance. When performed in rapid succession, this cycle allows the muscles to store some of the lost energy in the stretching phase for use during the contraction phase. Plyometrics is currently viewed as one of the best ways (if not the best way) to improve power. It is a growing practice, not only in power sports like football, and has been used to increase power in other areas. Power is similar to strength, except you are adding a time factor; that is, a person can drive their legs harder if they have more power in the moment of contraction and more speed in the contraction itself. It is not just the contraction of the muscle, but how fast will it contract.

A muscle will contract the fastest when it has been *loaded*, or stretched, first. A lineman will block harder if he crouches down a bit just before the drive, thus loading or stretching the thigh muscles and then contracting and pushing forward.

Plyometrics is the way to practice how to perform a power movement better. By shortening the time it takes for the muscles to contract, it results in more power.

However, I don't support use of such power training at beginner or intermediate levels, and coaches should probably avoid it altogether. At advanced levels, competition is such that players need to keep up with others and find a way to get an edge, so plyometric training may be unavoidable. At young ages, before fifteen, joints are still forming. Jumping form is not well developed, and powerful thrusts can lead to injury. If a kid can't squat twice his body weight, I'd stay away from it. Plus, it's just not that important. The following, however, are some plyometric drills, the first two of which do not yield a great stress on joints. The third should be reserved for advanced levels. Players should be warmed up before trying these drills.

Two-foot ankle hop. Keep the feet together. Remaining in one place, hop up and down using only the ankles and calves. Concentrate on getting as high as possible and explode off the floor as soon as possible after landing. (beginner level)

Rapid jumps. Stand under a hoop or another object that is within reach. Jump up and touch the object; alternate hands each time. Focus on jumping as high as possible and exploding back up very quickly after landing. (intermediate level)

Box jumps. This is a classic plyometric exercise. Place two boxes that are 1- to 2-feet high about 2 to 3 feet from each other. Make sure that they will support the player's weight. Step down from one box to the floor and immediately jump back up onto the

160

other box. Make sure the boxes will not move or slide; such boxes are sold in sporting goods stores. Repeat several times. Difficulty increases with height of the boxes. Jumping onto a soft surface such as a mat is preferable at first. Professional athletes jump with weights on their ankles or wearing weight jackets, but, again, those are the pros. (advanced level)

INJURIES

Football equipment today is vastly improved since my first edition of this book. At grade-school levels, the kids are smaller and don't hit with the same force as older, heavier players. Also, kids are usually quite resilient. Yet football is a full contact sport, and injuries do occur. There are things parents and coaches can do to reduce the probability of injury and to avoid compounding an injury that does occur.

The first thing parents and coaches should do is educate their players about the dangers of *spearing*—using the helmet to deliver a blow while blocking, tackling, or running with the ball. Spearing is illegal and is the most dangerous act in all of football. I'll discuss brain and spinal injuries in more detail later in this chapter. It's also useful to chat with the coach about this. Coaches usually are fully aware of spearing and instruct kids to keep their heads up, but it never hurts to increase a coach's sensitivity to this problem.

Another step is to inspect the equipment. Is the helmet padding intact? Does it fit properly? Are the chin straps snug? Are they frayed? Is the mouthpiece attached to the helmet? Does it fit? Are the shoulder pad straps and laces snug? Are hip, thigh, and tailbone pads in good shape? Are the knee pads okay?

How about the practice fields? Are there any stones or other protrusions? Are there any holes, ruts, or tracks? (This is how ankles get sprained.) If you see any, let the coach know. Perhaps you can get a few other parents together to fill any holes or remove any protrusions or other debris.

Finally, is there a trainer or someone qualified in first aid at practice? This is *very* important when the players scrimmage or otherwise engage in full-body contact. Most leagues require coaches to obtain licenses that expose them to first aid techniques. But is there someone who really knows what to do? If not, remember that parents can take a course and become quite knowledgeable. Perhaps a parent can volunteer as a trainer, although its best to have a fully trained medical professional.

I watched a team scrimmage just a few days before I wrote this chapter. A kid twisted his knee. The coach was short-handed for players and seemed more concerned about getting the kid back into the scrimmage than worrying about the extent of any injury. A few minutes later, the kid was back in the action, and after a play, I noticed he was limping a bit. The coach never looked at him! As a parent, it pays to attend a few practices to see how sensitive the coach is to injury. A good rule is that a player who complains of any injury to any joint cannot play for at least ten minutes to see if pain or swelling is still present.

No matter how well conditioned a team is, injuries can occur anytime. A common injury is a hamstring pull, but this usually doesn't occur until high school or later. Strained knees, ankles, and necks are the most common to football. Upper-leg (groin) strains, bloody noses, sprained wrists and forearms, jammed fingers, dislocations, and bruises also occur. Thankfully, broken bones are rare.

Abrasions occur often on the nose, although face gear protects the face very well. Abrasions also show up on the elbow, forearm, and lower leg. These cuts are the most likely to get infected. Wash the wound as soon as possible, with soap if it is handy. Apply a dressing when you can—the sooner the better. Put some antiseptic on it. If it gets red or oozes pus, see a physician.

Lacerations are deeper wounds. Unless bleeding is severe, wash the wound and apply direct pressure with a bandage to stop the bleeding. If it is severe or deep, seek first aid. Keep applying pressure and secure the dressing with a bandage (you can tie the knot right over the wound to reinforce the pressure). Immediately elevate the wound higher than the heart to help slow the bleeding. Remember, if the bandage over the wound gets blood-soaked, don't remove it; just apply a new dressing right over it. If the person has lost a lot of blood, you'll need to treat him for shock. Keep him warm with blankets, and call for help. If a laceration is major, a butterfly bandage will hold the skin together. Consult a physician immediately for stitches.

Contusions and bruises occur frequently. Apply ice quickly after taking care of any abrasions or lacerations. Ice arrests internal bleeding and prevents or lessens swelling. Ice is the best first aid available for nearly any swelling from bruises or sprains. Apply it very quickly. Do not move the child, especially if he is down due to a tough tackle or jolt. He could have a spinal injury and the slightest movement could do serious damage.

Sprained ankles, knees, and wrists should be immobilized. An ice pack should be applied immediately. Act as if there is a fracture until you're sure there isn't. Call an ambulance if there is any question in your mind. Get an X-ray to see if there is a break or other damage.

If there is a fracture, completely immobilize the child as soon as possible. There should be no movement at all. Comfort him, warm him with coats or blankets, and get medical help. Do not allow a child to be moved or cared for by anyone who is not medically trained. If the player is in the middle of the field during a championship game, the game can wait. Insist on this. Permanent damage can result from aggravating a break.

Heat exhaustion can occur during football practices or games, particularly early in the season during those sweltering August practice sessions. A body with heat exhaustion gets clammy and pale. Remove the child from the playing field, apply cool towels, and elevate the feet. If the body temperature is very high and pupils are contracted, you should suspect heat stroke. Call an ambulance and cool him down fast. Treat him for shock.

Knees injuries can occur. Often, the injury requires some sort of arthroscopic surgery to mend cartilage. Modern procedures are quite advanced and simple. Take the child to a knowledgeable sports doctor. Your team's coach or high-school athletic director will know one.

Tell players to play the game safely. Aggressiveness is okay, but they should never intentionally hurt someone. I play flag football frequently, and there are often one or two guys who take chances with the health of others. Don't encourage a child to grow up like them.

When an injury occurs, insist on rest. I've seen many kids rush back from a sprained ankle, only to have the injury plague them through the years. Don't let that happen. And make sure that a player wears an ankle brace from then on. There are excellent ankle braces on the market today.

The point is that injuries need time to heal right. If you give them that time, the future can hold many years of sports for the player. If you don't, his playing days could be over already.

CRITICAL INJURIES

If a child ever falls to the ground unconscious, see if anyone present has been trained as a first responder. Once it is clear that the child does not respond, the first move is to check for the vital signs: airway, breathing, and circulation, the ABCs of first aid. Send for an ambulance and let a trained person administer rescue breathing or CPR (cardiopulmonary resuscitation) if necessary. Try to stay calm and let the first responders do their job. In all my years of coaching four sports and playing even more, I've never seen CPR needed. I hope that you won't either.

Catastrophic spine and brain injuries among football players are rare and have decreased more in the past twenty years with improvements to equipment and with rules against head spearing. Yet, they do happen. This is obviously a most unpleasant subject, but it is important that you understand some of the details because many deadly injuries of the brain and paralyzing injuries of the spine are caused by earlier blows. A concerned and informed parent or coach could step in and prevent serious injury.

Many fans will recall the awful TV image in 1992 of Dennis Byrd of the New York Jets severely injuring himself by smashing headfirst into teammate Scott Mersereau's chest as they both attempted to tackle Kansas City Chief quarterback Dave Krieg. The image reminded me of a similar play nearly thirty years ago as I dove toward a running back at the line of scrimmage and collided headfirst with my own linebacker as the running back put on a spurt past us. It was the hardest blow I ever took, and I remember thinking that the lights would go out. I groggily got up and was able to collect myself. Fortunately, there was a penalty on the play, so I had time to figure out who and where I was. The linebacker was in the same state I was. I continued to play, but I should have been taken off the field.

While the neck bones are fragile, the neck muscles are quite strong and generally absorb the shock of most blows. With the head up, the upper-shoulder muscles and upper back help out. However, when a blow or jolt is taken by the top of the head (helmet), it goes down the spine, compresses the discs, and forces them to buckle. The spinal cord is like a rope made of millions of small strands carrying the information of the central nervous system. When this is bruised or damaged by the buckling spinal sheath, it's like a broken TV cable—no signal.

Head and neck injuries are reported by the National Collegiate Athletic Association (NCAA) survey of catastrophic football injuries. They occurred about twenty times a year nationwide in college and high school in the early 1970s. However, with improvements in equipment, bans on spearing, and better conditioning of the neck muscles, the incidents of permanent cervical spinal cord injury has been cut in half and is a bit more than one in two hundred thousand per year. Such injuries are even more rare at the grade-school level. Most of these injuries occur to defensive players during tackling or to those on kickoff teams.

This is not to say that every neck strain is a major injury. A fairly common injury is known as a *burner*. A group of physicians discussed this injury in the September 1991 issue of *The Physician and Sportsmedicine*. Burners are a temporary nerve dysfunction caused by a blow to the neck, head, or shoulder. They are like pinched nerves and arise from a sudden stretching of nerve channels. The player experiences a sharp pain—it can seem like an electric shock—followed by a burning sensation. The sensation can radiate down the arm and can be accompanied by a sharp reflex action. I know about burners because I had one in practice one day, going one-on-one with a big lineman. It felt like a buzzing in my lower neck and pain in my left arm. I had some occasional soreness there for years, especially after a lot of exercise. Burners usually go away, sometimes after a few minutes. However, players should always see a physician, and certainly should get a neck collar. Now that you know the symptoms, take control if it happens.

More serious than spinal injuries are possible injury to the head and brain. The *New York Times* published an article on January 18, 2007, *PRO FOOTBALL: Expert Ties Ex-Player's Suicide To Brain Damage From Football, that* reported on sustained brain damage from playing football, and that a medical examiner, in the case of former NFL player Andre Waters "determined that Mr. Waters's brain tissue had degenerated into that of an 85-year-old man with similar characteristics as those of early-stage Alzheimer's victims. [Neuropathologist] Dr. [Bennet] Omalu said he believed that the damage was either caused or drastically expedited by successive concussions Mr. Waters, 44, had sustained playing football."

Any level of confusion or headache brought on by a blow to the head should receive *immediate* medical attention. Get the player out of the game! Players who sustain a severe blow to the head should be removed for at least twenty minutes, and they should not be allowed to return to the game if any confusion or amnesia persists during that time. If a player ever loses consciousness, he should go straight to the hospital.

Perhaps more than with any other sport, attention must be paid to the players' health. While my experience is that the game is safe, as a coach, it is your responsibility to be aware of how the kids feel, of any injuries, or of any health issues. If you get a hunch that its not safe to proceed, whether it's a wet field, a very hot day in August, or a kid with a slight limp, follow that hunch and take appropriate action. Remember, it's just a game!

10 COACHES' AND PARENTS' CHECKLIST

If you are a parent, watch your son when you go to a practice or a game. Look over the checkpoints on these lists and evaluate his performance. If you are a coach, bring the lists to practices; they will help you to focus your attention on possible problem areas.

DESIRE

- ❏ Drive for the ball.
- ❏ Hustle; play until the whistle.
- ❏ Never quit.

BLOCKING

STANCE

- ❏ Drop sharply from ready to set positions.
- ❏ Set position—shoulders are low and coiled.
- ❏ Legs are shoulder-width or more apart.
- ❏ Weight is moderately forward on hand.
- ❏ Down hand is inside back foot and just forward of shoulder, resting on the three interior fingers' knuckles, thumb is back.
- ❏ Legs are bent so the back is parallel to the ground.
- ❏ Tail is not higher than the shoulders.
- ❏ Head is up.
- ❏ Back is straight, not curved.
- ❏ Neck is bulled, eyes are forward; don't give away any clues.

CHARGE

- ❏ Explode instantly with the snap.
- ❏ Drive forward with both feet.

- ❏ Stay low, legs wide, knees bent.
- ❏ Raise forearms toward opponent's chest, elbows out.
- ❏ Angle, don't step, to opposite side.
- ❏ Adjust for stunts.

JOLT

- ❏ Slam shoulder into opponent hard.
- ❏ Drive, don't lunge.
- ❏ Straighten legs on contact.
- ❏ Keep eyes open wide, head up.
- ❏ Sustain the block.
- ❏ Keep legs wide.
- ❏ Bring back leg up under the body.
- ❏ Move into the opponent's pressure.
- ❏ Drive forward with short, choppy steps.
- ❏ Turn opponent away and then back toward the line of scrimmage.

SPECIALTY BLOCKS

- ❏ Trap.
- ❏ Stalk block.
- ❏ Cross block.
- ❏ Double-team.
- ❏ Pass block.

TACKLING

STANCE

- ❏ Similar to a blocker's, but more weight forward.
- ❏ Low under the opponent.
- ❏ Head up.
- ❏ Inside foot back.
- ❏ Search for keys.
- ❏ Crouch if in a standing stance.

TACKLING TECHNIQUES

- ❏ Explode off the snap.
- ❏ Neutralize the blocker's charge with the shoulder. Give a jolt of your own.

❏ Shiver: Both palms thrust up into opponent's shoulder pads to keep him at bay.

❏ Stay under control.

❏ Drop to all fours if not blocked; stack things up.

❏ Shed blocker at moment ball carrier commits to one side.

FOCUS AND WRAP

❏ Drop or dip low.

❏ Focus on the belt.

❏ Have legs wide and balanced.

❏ Drive shoulder into thigh; jolt.

❏ Wrap arms tightly around the runner; try to smack the ball.

❏ Bring hips in and legs up quickly.

❏ Lift, drive, and then bring him down.

❏ If off-balance, tackle him any way possible.

PASSING

QUARTERBACK BASICS

❏ Good form is essential under pressure.

❏ Size up the defense; where are the seams?

❏ Secure the snap with passing hand on top, fingers spread.

❏ Retreat quickly; practice the footwork.

❏ Hold the ball high.

❏ Step forward into pocket.

GRIP

❏ Snug, but not a squeeze.

❏ Fingers spread wide, touching ball along the entire length.

❏ Hand back of center; pinky is mid-ball.

❏ Laces under last joint of fingers.

❏ Some space between palm and ball.

❏ Free hand protects ball.

RELEASE

❏ Stand erect, survey the field.

❏ Hold the ball high.

- Hit player as he breaks and is in a seam between defenders.
- Don't take too big a step; step toward target.
- Snap the wrist; ball rolls off fingertips.
- Long pass: Tilt the nose of the ball up and err long.
- Short pass: Nose of the ball even or down a bit; snap and throw hard and err low and short.
- Jump pass: Adjust lead, release at top of jump, try to get some forward momentum.

RECEIVING

FUNDAMENTALS
- Don't let the opponent delay you at the line.
- Run directly at the defender.
- Cut into a pattern when the defender changes momentum to backpedal.
- Make a two- or three-step fake and quickly change direction.
- Stay under control; save a bit of speed.
- React to the ball.
- Don't ignore the passer; look to him.
- Focus on the ball.
- Don't reach too soon.
- Have soft hands, fingers curled and spread.
- Catch it high, at front point or tip of the ball.
- Watch the ball all the way into the hands.
- Try to catch the ball while body is in the air.
- Recover and tackle if intercepted.
- Tuck the ball in before running.
- Change direction immediately.

RUNNING

STANCE
- Have feet spread wide outside shoulders.
- Put very little weight on down hand.
- Focus straight ahead, don't tip off the defense.

PIVOT AND SNAP

❏ Pivot first before stepping.

❏ Snap head and shoulders.

❏ Push off balls of the feet.

❏ Make sure first step is a large one with foot on same side as play action.

❏ Look at the hole to see what is developing, and let the quarterback worry about getting you the ball.

❏ Have outside arm down across stomach, palm up; the other arm has the elbow up across the chest on dive plays.

❏ Curl both hands around the tips of the ball.

❏ Carry the ball securely; jam it into the pocket between the upper arm and ribs, forearm to the underside, fingers spread around the front top.

❏ Carry the ball in the arm farthest from the tackler, usually the arm closest to the nearest sideline.

❏ Run with power; run hard.

RUNNING MANEUVERS

❏ Stiff-arm: Just as tackler launches, place palm on shoulder or on top of helmet, lock arm, hop a bit on contact to maintain balance.

❏ Step out: Jab and then step or leap sharply away.

❏ Pivot or spin: Give a leg and take it away with 360-degree spin, then change direction.

❏ Cross over: Lean and lift leg away from tackler.

SPECIALTIES

SNAP TO QUARTERBACK

❏ Feet wide, hips high, legs even.

❏ Weight moderately on the ball.

❏ Head and arm may be in neutral zone.

❏ Tilt ball as needed.

❏ Timing is critical.

❏ Quick, firm snap to the hands, laces to fingertips.

❏ Step forward with the snap.

❏ Angle head and jolt.

SNAP FOR PUNTS AND PLACE KICKS

❏ Hold ball up front with a passer's grip.

❏ Raise the front point of the ball.

❏ Have weight forward moderately on the ball.

❏ Guide ball with the left hand; this hand leaves the ball first.

❏ Brace and step forward with the snap.

❏ Drive ball back with quick snapping action.

❏ Aim for belt of the punter or hands of the place-kick holder.

❏ Snap with speed; time is precious—take as little as possible.

❏ Focus on the snap, not the opponent.

PUNTING

❏ Look only at the ball as it is snapped.

❏ Have feet parallel, weight on left foot.

❏ Extend arms outward, palms down and inward, thumbs up, fingers spread.

❏ Stand erect, hands soft, body relaxed.

❏ Let the snap come all the way to the hands.

❏ Withdraw and soften hands to receive the ball.

❏ Place the laces up; right hand back cradling the ball.

❏ Serve, don't drop, ball to foot; use the right hand (if right-handed).

❏ Point tip of ball down and inside a bit.

❏ Contact with belly of ball. Spiral results if ball is kicked with right side of the foot, to the right of shoelaces, a hair off-center.

❏ End-over-end kick results if ball is kicked directly on the instep.

❏ Snap the locked ankle forward to give power and distance.

❏ Point the toe forward.

❏ Concentrate on point of contact.

❏ Drive ball back with quick snapping action.

❏ Follow through enough to pull the body forward a hop.

PLACE-KICKING

❏ Take two or three steps, depending on distance.

❏ Kick soccer style.

❏ Stand with legs nearly even, leaning forward on front foot while waiting for snap.

❏ Approach ball in a quarter-circle motion.

171

❏ Plant toes of free foot even with back of ball, a few inches to the side, pointing at the target.

❏ Concentrate on point of contact.

RECEIVING PUNTS AND KICKOFFS

❏ Judge where the ball will land.

❏ Catch the ball while moving forward.

❏ Have arms raised outward, upward a bit, palms up, fingers spread, hands fairly close together.

❏ Catch with hands and bring ball quickly into body.

❏ Soften hands and body for the catch.

APPENDIX: SUMMARY OF PENALTIES

LOSS OF 5 YARDS

1. Failure to properly wear required equipment during a down
2. Delay of game
3. Failure to properly wear required equipment prior to snap
4. Illegal substitution
5. Encroachment
6. Free kick infraction
7. Invalid or illegal fair catch signal
8. False start or any illegal act by snapper
9. Fewer than seven on offensive line or a numbering violation
10. Illegal formation or procedure at snap
11. Illegal motion or shift
12. Illegal handling ball forward (also loss of down)
13. Illegal forward pass (if by offense, loss of down also)
14. Intentional grounding (also loss of down)
15. Ineligible receiver downfield
16. Helping runner
17. Attendant illegally on field
18. Non-player outside of the team box but not on field
19. Unintentionally grabbing an opponent's protective face gear (facemask)

LOSS OF 10 YARDS

1. Illegal blocking technique
2. Illegal use of hands
3. Interlocked blocking

4. Holding

5. Runner grasping a teammate

6. Striking blocker's head with hand(s)

LOSS OF 15 YARDS

1. Fair catch interference

2. Illegal block after valid or invalid fair catch signal

3. Forward pass interference (also loss of down if by offense; a first down if by defense). If intentional or unsportsmanlike, an additional 15 yards

4. Illegal block below the waist

5. Clipping

6. Chop block

7. Tripping

8. Charging into an opponent obviously out of the play

9. Piling, hurdling, unnecessary roughness, personal fouls

10. Grasping opponent's face protector or any helmet opening

11. Butt block, face tackle, or spear

12. Roughing the passer (also a first down)

13. Roughing the kicker or holder (also a first down)

14. Unsportsmanlike conduct by player or non-player

15. Illegal participation (twelve players on the field)

16. Illegal kicking or batting the ball

17. Non-player illegally on field

Note: Striking, kicking, kneeling, or any act, if unduly rough or flagrant, may result in player disqualification.

GLOSSARY: TALKING FOOTBALL

Audible: A play called audibly at the line of scrimmage, changing the play called in the huddle.

Backfield: The quarterback and running backs constitute the offensive backfield. There are tailbacks (deep in the backfield), flankerbacks (spread outside of the end), wing-backs (spread out behind the end), single or lone backs (when there is only one running back behind the quarterback), and others based on regional terminology. The defensive backfield is called the *secondary*.

Bat: In a few instances, batting a ball by hand is legal. A player can bat a pass, kick, or fumble in flight if he is attempting to block. He can also bat a kicked ball forward before he or the ball goes into the opponent's end zone to avoid a touchback.

Blindside: The side of the quarterback opposite to the side of the field he is looking at. He often does not see an approaching tackler in his blindside until too late.

Blitz: A defensive move by a member of the secondary (linebacker, cornerback, or safety) in which the player leaves his zone and rushes through a gap in the offensive line toward the quarterback, hoping to tackle him or the ball carrier behind the line of scrimmage for a loss of yardage. The move has some risk because the blitzer's defensive zone is left uncovered.

Blocking: The act of impeding a defensive player by moving him from the path of the ball carrier or interfering with his ability to make a tackle. Types of blocks include: *cross-body blocks*, in which a blocker hurls his body horizontally across the chest of a defender; *shoulder blocks*, or jolts; *open field blocks*, in which a player blocks a defender downfield; and *screens*, in which a blocker simply gets between a defender and the ball carrier. A running back who blocks well is often called a blocking back. Defenders also try to block or bat punts and place kicks.

175

Bootleg: A deception move in which the quarterback fakes a handoff to a running back and then, hiding the ball by his hip, runs wide around the end to gain yardage. Often, the quarterback runs casually at first, pretending he doesn't have the ball to perpetuate the fake, and then suddenly speeds up.

Buck: Running hard into the middle of the defensive line in an attempt to break through it, often on a short-yardage situation.

Buttonhook: A route in which the receiver runs straight ahead for 5 to 7 yards, then wheels and turns to face the quarterback for a pass. The buttonhook is often a timing pass and the ball meets the receiver as soon as he stops and turns. A great fake move is for the receiver, just after he turns and as the defender is approaching, to instead break downfield. It's a great play and works if the quarterback has time to let the fake buttonhook develop.

Center: The offensive lineman who snaps (or centers) the ball to the quarterback. He is usually found in the center of the offensive line and generally has a number in the 50s.

Chain gang: A group of three field assistants, one of whom is responsible for holding the *down marker*, a tall pole with cards displayed on the top to signify which down it is. This person places the pole on the new line of scrimmage on each play. The other two people handle the *chains*, which are two tall poles, separated by a 10-foot chain. The distance between these poles is the distance that must be covered to get a first down. At youth levels, chain gang members are parents who are pressed into service along the sideline.

Clipping: Blocking an opponent from behind and below the waist outside a free-blocking zone (see *free-blocking zone*). Clipping carries a 15-yard penalty. If the block is above the waist, the penalty is 5 yards and the block is called *illegal use of hands*.

Clothesline: An illegal tackle made by extending the arm in front of a ball carrier's head or neck.

Counter: A play pattern in which the offensive backs flow in one direction, then one cuts back to run the ball in the other direction.

Cutback: A runner's move when he crosses the line of scrimmage in a certain direction and then cuts back in the other direction as he penetrates the defense. A cutback is like a counter except that it occurs spontaneously and after the runner crosses the line of scrimmage.

Dead ball spot: The spot under the foremost point of the ball when it becomes dead by rule—that is, when the runner steps on or over the sideline or when his knee touches the ground. In professional football, the ball is dead when the runner's knee touches the ground as a result of contact with an opponent. If a runner slips in the pros, he can get up again and run if he was not touched. In youth ball through college, a runner is down if his knee hits the ground, regardless of whether or not he's been touched by an opponent. The official *spots* the ball at the end of each play. Spotting the ball is not an exact science and it can cause controversy since the spot often determines whether a team keeps the ball or loses possession.

Delay of game: A penalty called when a team takes too long to start play.

Dime defense: Use of six defensive backs; used in college and professional football.

Dive: A running play up the middle in the gap between the center and the guard. It is a quick-moving play that is usually run by a strong back, the fullback.

Down: A down is a play. A team gets four downs to move the ball 10 yards. If they succeed, they get four more downs. If they fail, the other team gets the ball.

Draw: A play that tries to draw the defense into the backfield by delaying the handoff to the running back. Then, as a defender charges, he is hit in the side by a pre-designed trap block and the runner is free to advance. The delay gives the blocker time to run along the line of scrimmage and get to the defender.

Dummy: Players who hold dummy or blocking pads in practice to allow blockers to run through their plays and work on blocking.

Eligible receiver: Not all players are eligible to receive passes. Offensive backs and the two players on either side of the line of scrimmage are eligible. If they have a number on their backs between 50 and 79, they need to report to the referee that they are eligible (and will otherwise also be on one end of the line of scrimmage). The reporting is so the referee can see where they line up. Interior offensive lineman are never eligible receivers.

Encroachment: A 5-yard penalty for having any part of the body inside the neutral zone at the snap of the ball.

End: The offensive or defensive player who positions himself at either end of the front line. On offense, an end in close to the rest of the line is called a tight end; otherwise, he's a split end. Ends usually have numbers in the 80s.

End zone: The area covering 10 yards past each goal line. A pass caught in the end zone is a touchdown. The goalposts are located at the back of the end zone.

Extra point (point after touchdown): The field goal attempt made immediately after a touchdown. This field goal is only worth one point. At youth levels, the point after touchdown may be attempted from the 3-yard line. If the ball is place-kicked through the goalposts, two points are scored in Pop Warner play.

Fair catch: By raising his hand above his head quickly and clearly, a player may receive a punt or place kick without being tackled. He may not, however, advance the ball, and a muffed catch results in a live ball.

Field goal: An attempt to score three points by place-kicking the ball through the uprights of the goalpost. When a team has a fourth down and is close to the goal line, they can opt to kick a field goal instead of going for a touchdown. It doesn't happen often at the youth level because the kids rarely place kick with accuracy.

First down: The first play in each series of four chances to move the ball 10 yards. When a team makes 10 yards they are awarded another first down, or *first and 10*. The chains move and they have four more chances (downs) to move another 10 yards.

Facemask: A penalty given when a tackler grabs the facemask of the ball carrier. It's a 15-yard penalty, unless the grab is only momentary and unintentional, in which case it is a 5-yard penalty.

Flag: A yellow penalty cloth that an official keeps in his back pocket and throws in the air to designate a rule violation.

Flat: The area of the field near the line of scrimmage along the sideline.

Flea-flicker: A play in which the quarterback hands off to a running back who then flicks the ball *back* to the quarterback for a pass play. The objective is to fool the defense into thinking it is a running play so they will leave pass receivers unguarded.

Forward progress: The point at which the ball is placed after a play, marking the forward-most point of a runner's progress before he was involuntarily knocked backward. If a receiver backs up voluntarily, he loses any forward progress that he had gained beyond the point of the tackle.

Free-blocking zone: A rectangular area extending 4 yards laterally and 3 yards forward and behind each scrimmage line from the point of the ball. In this zone, an offensive player who was stationary at the snap and all defensive players may contact an opponent below the waist or from the rear.

Fullback: A running back. Usually he is the strongest running back, used for short-yardage dives up the middle. Fullbacks are also used heavily to block for another running back. Fullbacks usually have numbers in the 30s.

Fumble: Dropping the football before the play ends, usually due to a hard tackle. A fumble cannot be caused by contact with the ground. A fumble is a live ball; whoever recovers it gains possession.

Gaps: The spaces between offensive linemen through which the ball is carried. Defensive players try to fill the gaps.

Goal line: The white lines marking the ends of the 100-yard playing surface. If at any point of the ball breaks the vertical plane of this line, a touchdown is scored.

Goalpost: One of the two uprights of the goal that is situated in the center of each end line. The goalposts are connected by a crossbar that is 10 feet above the ground and 23 feet, 4 inches long. The uprights may be 4 inches thick and extend no less than 10 feet above the crossbar. The lower goalposts (if the goal is H-shaped) or post (if the goal is Y-shaped—slingshot), must be padded. A wind directional streamer may be atop one of the uprights.

Guard: An interior lineman on offense who lines up next to the center. The middle person on the defensive line is called a *nose guard*. Guards usually wear numbers in the 60s.

Halfbacks: The faster running backs, usually lined up behind and to one side of the quarterback for wide running plays. Halfbacks usually wear numbers in the 40s.

Halftime: After two ten-minute quarters (at the youth level) there is a fifteen-minute halftime break. The pros recently reduced this break to twelve minutes to speed up the game.

Hash marks: Also called the *inbounds line*, these markings are 24 inches in length and form two broken lines down the field, 53 feet, 4 inches from each sideline, dividing the field longitudinally into thirds. When a ball goes out of bounds or is downed near a sideline, it is centered on the nearest hash mark for the next play. This gives the team some running room to each side on every play.

Huddle: Players gather before each play in a circle or other formation to receive the play instructions from the quarterback.

Incompletion: A forward pass that is not caught or not possessed by the receiver for a full step.

Ineligible receiver: A player that is not allowed to be an intended target for the quarterback. Only the ends or backs may be downfield to receive a pass. This violation often occurs on punts when an interior lineman breaks downfield before the ball is punted.

Intentional grounding: When a quarterback has no receiver open and is under pressure, he often throws the ball away, either out of bounds or to an open area. The rules call this intentional grounding. It is a 10-yard penalty, unless a receiver was nearby or the quarterback was out of his pocket, in which case there is no penalty.

Interception: A pass reception by the defense.

Interference: Called against the offense or defense for interfering with a player who is trying to receive a pass, usually by bumping or grabbing his hands before the ball gets to him. Incidental contact between two players who are both looking at and trying to catch a pass is not interference. The judgment is always whether the player was playing the receiver or the ball.

Kickoff: The free kick that starts the game and the second half. It also occurs after each touchdown or successful field goal and is kicked from the kicking team's 40-yard line. A *kickoff return* is the formation used by the receiving team to return the ball.

Lateral: A sideways or backward pass. It can be thrown at any time from any place on the field and usually is used to avoid a tackle.

Linebackers: The defensive personnel immediately behind defensive linemen. Linebackers are usually both agile and strong, and they are great tacklers. They often wear numbers in the 50s and 90s.

Man-to-man: A pass defense term that designates individual coverage. Each defensive back is assigned to stay with a specific offensive receiver on a pass play.

Muff: An unsuccessful attempt to catch a punt or kickoff or to recover a fumble.

Neutral zone: An imaginary belt across the field formed by the front and back points of the football as it rests with its foremost tip on the line of scrimmage. No one, except the center, may be in the neutral zone before the snap.

180

Officials: There are usually four officials in a high-school crew. I've seen Pop Warner games with only two or three. The *referee* is in charge—he keeps score, supervises the conduct of the game, and keeps the game clock. He decides differences of opinion. He usually lines up on the offensive side of scrimmage and primarily decides forward progress of the ball. The *umpire* is responsible for penalty administration and lines up on the defensive side of scrimmage. The *linesman* covers action in the neutral zone and stands on the line of scrimmage. He looks for pass interference on his side of the field. The *line judge* is on the opposite side from the linesman. The official signals are found in figure on pages 182–184.

Offsides: Crossing the line of scrimmage before the ball is snapped. The penalty for this violation is a loss of 5 yards.

Off-tackle: The gap between the defensive tackle and the defensive end; it's a popular place for running plays.

Onside kick: A short, bouncing kickoff aimed to travel only 10 yards so the kicking team can attempt to recover it. The kicking team is not allowed to touch the ball until it has traveled at least 10 yards. This is usually attempted late in the game by a losing team as a desperation play and as an alternative to doing a traditional kickoff.

Option: A popular play at youth and high-school levels, and even in some colleges. The quarterback sweeps around an end with another running back just off his outside shoulder. He can keep the ball or lateral it to the other back, depending on how the defense reacts. An *option pass play* is a sweep by a halfback who has the option of passing the ball or continuing the run, again depending on how the defense reacts. *Triple option plays* include an optional belly dive before the option sweep.

Penalties: A penalty is the consequence of an infraction of the rules of football. It is measured in increments of 5, 10, or 15 yards against the team that committed the foul. A penalty may be awarded from the place of infraction (at the spot of the foul), the line of scrimmage, or the end of the play, depending on the infraction. It may also be declined by the other team if it would be to their benefit, meaning they would get possession of the ball, or if they scored on the play. See the appendix for a summary of penalties.

Pile-up: Piling on a tackled ballplayer is illegal. However, the forward momentum of tacklers often carries several to a pile-up.

OFFICIAL SIGNALS

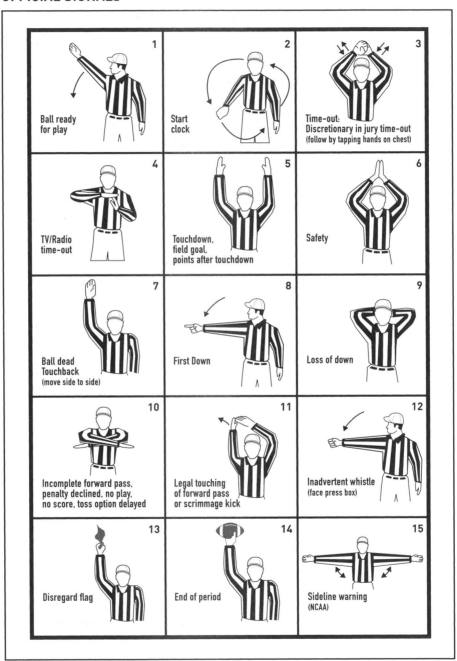

1 Ball ready for play

2 Start clock

3 Time-out: Discretionary in jury time-out (follow by tapping hands on chest)

4 TV/Radio time-out

5 Touchdown, field goal, points after touchdown

6 Safety

7 Ball dead Touchback (move side to side)

8 First Down

9 Loss of down

10 Incomplete forward pass, penalty declined, no play, no score, toss option delayed

11 Legal touching of forward pass or scrimmage kick

12 Inadvertent whistle (face press box)

13 Disregard flag

14 End of period

15 Sideline warning (NCAA)

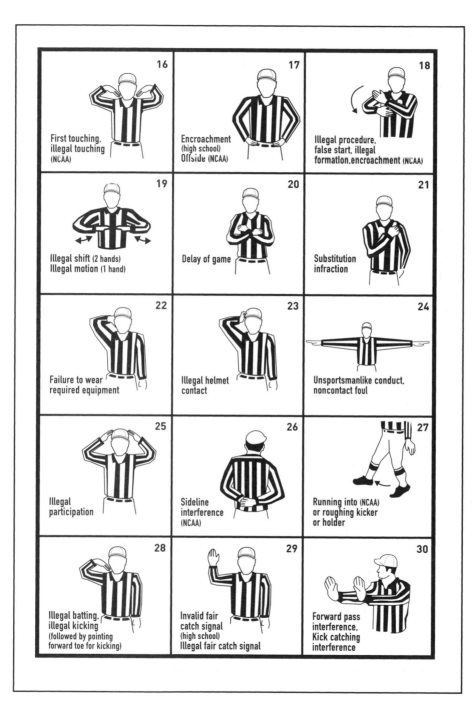

16 First touching, illegal touching (NCAA)

17 Encroachment (high school) Offside (NCAA)

18 Illegal procedure, false start, illegal formation, encroachment (NCAA)

19 Illegal shift (2 hands) Illegal motion (1 hand)

20 Delay of game

21 Substitution infraction

22 Failure to wear required equipment

23 Illegal helmet contact

24 Unsportsmanlike conduct, noncontact foul

25 Illegal participation

26 Sideline interference (NCAA)

27 Running into (NCAA) or roughing kicker or holder

28 Illegal batting, illegal kicking (followed by pointing forward toe for kicking)

29 Invalid fair catch signal (high school) Illegal fair catch signal

30 Forward pass interference, Kick catching interference

183

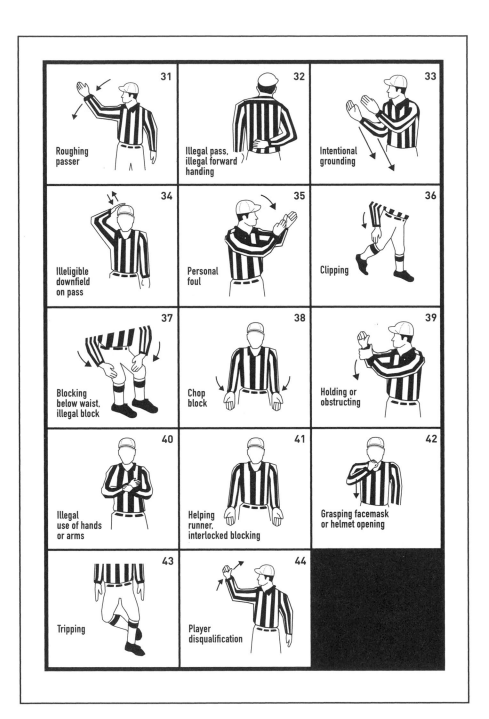

31 Roughing passer

32 Illegal pass, illegal forward handing

33 Intentional grounding

34 Illeligible downfield on pass

35 Personal foul

36 Clipping

37 Blocking below waist, illegal block

38 Chop block

39 Holding or obstructing

40 Illegal use of hands or arms

41 Helping runner, interlocked blocking

42 Grasping facemask or helmet opening

43 Tripping

44 Player disqualification

Pitchout: A play designed to get a halfback to the outside of the field very quickly. On a *sweep play*, the ball is pitched to a halfback as he darts to the outside.

Place kick: Kicking a ball in a kickoff, a field goal, or a point after touchdown when the ball is held in place, either by a tee or by another teammate.

Play action pass: A pass play preceded by a faked handoff to a running back, designed to throw off the defense.

Platoon: Having different players on the offensive team than those on the defense. At youth levels, the best players play both ways.

Pocket: An area formed by the offensive pass blockers in front and to the side of the quarterback in a pass play. The purpose of the pocket is to protect the quarterback and to give him more time to throw the ball. When the quarterback is in the pocket, he cannot throw the ball away intentionally, or he will be called for intentional grounding.

Point after touchdown (PAT): See *extra point*.

Post pass: A deep pass across the middle, toward the goalpost. A very deep pass thrown in desperation is also called a *Hail Mary* or a *bomb*.

Punt: A ball kicked to the opponent by dropping it onto the foot. This usually is the method for exchanging possession on fourth down.

Pursuit: The defensive act of pursuing the ball carrier on an intercept angle, even if the play goes away from the defender.

Quarter: The game is divided into four time periods called quarters, usually ten minutes each at pre-high-school levels. There is a one- or two-minute period between quarters and a fifteen-minute halftime. High school games are for four twelve-minute quarters.

Quarterback: The offensive captain who calls the plays. He takes the snap and either hands off the ball to a running back or passes it. The quarterback usually wears a number from 1 to 19.

Razzle-dazzle: Intricate or funny play patterns, such as end around, reverse, flea-flicker or option. These involve tricky handoffs and often take a lot of precision but can break for big plays.

Replay: A videotaped copy of a football play. Replays are used in the pros and in college games to review an official's call.

Reverse: A play in which a running back runs to one side, pulling the defense with him, and then hands off the ball to another player going the other way.

Roll-out: Instead of staying in the pass protection *pocket*, an agile quarterback can run off to one side to gain time for his receivers to get open for a pass. This is a *scramble* if not designed ahead of time.

Sack: Tackling a quarterback behind the line of scrimmage before he has gotten rid of the ball.

Safety: (a) The deepest defensive back. (b) A tackle in a team's own end zone resulting in two points and a free kick to the opponent. A safety is also awarded if a ball is fumbled out of bounds or a ball carrier steps out of bounds, in a team's own end zone.

Scramble: The move a quarterback often makes to avoid onrushing tacklers when his protection breaks down. It involves running out of the pocket.

Screen pass: A play that allows the defensive line to rush the quarterback freely as a ploy. The quarterback then lofts a short pass over the charging defenders to a receiver who is positioned just behind the waiting offensive linemen.

Scrimmage: (a) The imaginary line across the field that runs through the point of the front tip of the ball. (b) A practice football game.

Secondary: The defensive backfield. It consists of safeties, cornerbacks, and linebackers.

Shift: Offensive backs and defenders are allowed to shift position and change alignment, individually or as a unit, before the ball is snapped. Offensive players must be set for one second before the snap (one player may legally be in motion as long as they were originally lined up behind the line of scrimmage).

Shiver: A useful defensive weapon, thrusting the hands forward, palms forward, into a blocker's shoulders to keep him at bay and thus not allowing him access to the defender's body.

Shoestring tackle: A tackle that occurs by a defender wrapping his arms around the ball carrier's ankles. It is preferable to tackle hard with the shoulder, but when the ball carrier is breaking away, the defensive player should grab for the feet.

Shotgun: An offensive formation in which the quarterback lines up 4 to 5 yards behind the center to receive the snap. This is used on obvious passing situations and helps the quarterback gain a few seconds. Since he need not drop back, he can more readily focus on the secondary and the pass pattern.

Sidelines: The white stripes lengthwise down the sides of the field. These lines are out of bounds to any body part.

Signals: The hiking cadence and instructions called by a quarterback at the line of scrimmage. A typical one is "Down, green, 242, set, hike-one, hike-two, hike-three." "Down" signifies that the team should get in the ready position. "Green," or any color, may be a code that signals if the play will be changed and is followed by the new play. The "set" signal gets the linemen into set position. The ball is hiked on a predetermined number called in the huddle.

Slant: A block to one side or a running play off-tackle or off-guard.

Snap: The backward hike of the ball between the legs the center to the quarterback or punter, place-kick holder. Sometimes the snap is to a player about 6 feet behind the center (such as the quarterback in a shotgun formation), or to a punter who stands back 3 to 4 yards or farther. These are called *long snaps*.

Spin move: A move by a running back as he is about to be tackled. With a good spin, a back can break free from a mediocre tackle.

Stance: The position of a player when the ball is snapped. Stances are designed to ready each person for his particular job, and the stances vary according to that task.

Stiff-arm: A useful weapon for a running back or receiver who is running with the ball is to stiff-arm, palms outward, onto the shoulder of a would-be tackler. A "hop" upon contact can often launch a runner, using the tackler's momentum, for several feet.

Stunts: Defensive moves to confuse blocking assignments by having linemen switch charging lanes when the ball is snapped.

Submarine: A low, diving defensive line move to get under a block and into a gap. The player then pulls his legs up under him quickly to meet the ball carrier.

Substitution: The substitution rules are fairly unrestricted. Any number of players may enter or leave between downs. No more than eleven players may be on the field at one time, although it is not illegal to have fewer. Eleven players are needed to start, but not to finish, a game.

Sweep: A running play designed to have the runner go wide laterally in an effort to run around the defense.

Tackle: (a) A lineman on offense or defense who plays inside the end. Linemen are usually the biggest players on the team. Their numbers are usually in the 70s. (b) The act of bringing a ball carrier to the ground.

Tailback: The deepest running back, that is, the one who lines up farthest from the line of scrimmage.

Timeout: Either side may stop the clock after any play three times per half. This is usually done by the team in possession of the ball to delay the half from ending so they have a chance to score. It's also used to talk things over before an important play. In youth levels, it's often used to stop the twenty-five-second clock from expiring while waiting for a player to get back on the field.

Timing pass: A prearranged pass pattern in which the quarterback throws to an area before the receiver actually turns or stops. It is usually too sophisticated for most youth teams.

Touchback: A punt or kickoff that goes into the end zone and is downed there by the team who will take possession. A touchback also occurs when a fumbled ball is recovered or a pass is intercepted in the offensive end zone by the defense and no attempt is made to run it out. In all instances, the team gets possession of the ball on their own 20-yard line.

Touchdown: Breaking the plane of the goal line with the ball. This can be achieved by running the ball over the goal line or by catching a pass in the end zone. It is the primary objective of the football game. It's worth six points. After a touchdown, a team is allowed one play, with the clock stopped, to get a point after touchdown.

Trapping: Blocking a player from the side after allowing him to advance beyond the line of scrimmage.

Twenty-five-second clock: The time between plays given for a team with possession to run another play. If this time expires, the offense is charged with a delay of game penalty of 5 yards.

Two-point conversion: After a touchdown, there is the option to go for one extra point or two. From the high-school level up to the pros, a two-point conversion is throwing or running the ball into the end zone on the play immediately after scoring the touchdown as opposed to kicking a field goal. In youth-level games, two points are usually given for kicking the field goal instead of running the play because it is more difficult for kids to kick the ball than run a play.

Unbalanced line: An offensive line with more linemen on one side of the center than on the other.

Wingback: A running back who lines up outside the offensive end.

Zone defense: When the pass defense protects a certain territory rather than defending man-to-man.

INDEX

190

MORE GREAT SPORTS TITLES
FROM BETTERWAY BOOKS!

Coaching Youth Basketball, third edition

The Guide for Coaches, Parents and Athletes

By John P. McCarthy, Jr.

This book covers all of basketball's fundamentals and gives coaching tips for every aspect of the game including: dribbling and passing skills; proper shooting technique for all types of shots; offensive concepts and plays for beginner and intermediate players; defensive tactics for getting the ball back; the responsibilities of centers, forwards, and guards; and how to work together as a team.

ISBN-13: 978-1-55870-790-0
ISBN-10: 1-55870-790-5
7x9, pb, 208 p, # Z0529

Coaching Youth Baseball, third edition

The Guide for Coaches, Parents and Athletes

By John P. McCarthy, Jr.

This book covers all of baseball's fundamentals and gives coaching tips for every aspect of the game including: fielding and throwing; proper batting techniques for all types of hits, including bunts; key concepts like using a cutoff; baserunning, sliding, and base coaching; the responsibilities of each position on the field; and even how to coach tee-ball.

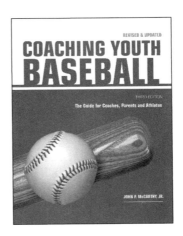

ISBN-13: 978-1-55870-793-1
ISBN-10: 1-55870-793-X
7x9, pb, 176 p, #Z0567

Coaching Youth Soccer, second edition

**The Guide for Coaches, Parents
and Athletes**
By John P. McCarthy, Jr.

This book covers all of soccer's fundamentals and gives coaching tips for every aspect of the game including: proper kicking, passing, and trapping techniques; dribbling, juggling, and headers; the responsibilities of each position on the field; defensive and offensive strategies; and rules and regulations for standard and small-sided games.

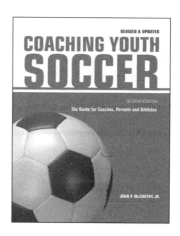

ISBN-13: 978-1-55870-794-8
ISBN-10: 1-55870-794-8
7x9, pb, 160 p, #Z0565

Youth Volleyball, second edition

**The Guide for Coaches, Parents
and Athletes**
By Sharkie Zartman

This book offers aspiring coaches and parents everything they need to understand and coach both boys and girls volleyball. Author Sharkie Zartman guides you through the ins and outs of the ultimate team sport, covering new serving rules, the rally scoring system, the libero position, the fundamentals, and more.

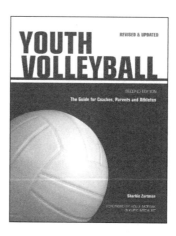

ISBN-13: 978-1-55870-787-0
ISBN-10: 1-55870-787-5
7x9, pb, 208 p, #Z0528

The Art of Doubles, second edition

Winning Tennis Strategies and Drills

By Pat Blaskower

Whether you're trying to improve your doubles game or are just getting started playing tennis with a partner, *The Art of Doubles* is the book for you. Author Pat Blaskower is your personal coach, guiding and encouraging you and your partner to play winning tennis. The book includes detailed court diagrams that show you how to execute offense, defense, and tactical plays; checklists that summarize the most important points of each chapter; and on-court drills to help you improve and refine your skills.

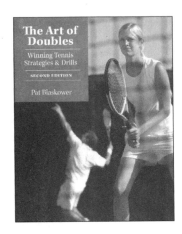

ISBN-13: 978-1-55870-823-5
ISBN-10: 1-55870-823-5
7x9, pb, 224 p, #Z1321

Basketball Drills, Plays, and Strategies
A Comprehensive Resource for Coaches
By Clint M. Adkins, Steven R. Bain, Edward A. Dreyer, Robert A. Starkey

This guide offers step-by-step illustrations and instructions for every practice drill *and* game play a basketball coach needs for a successful season. Not only will this book help coaches keep practice interesting and instructive, but it also helps coaches learn and understand a variety of plays to use in games. From offenses, to inbounds plays, to press breaks and last-second shots, this book will give coaches a wide variety of options when it's crunch time.

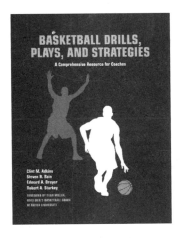

ISBN-13: 978-1-55870-810-5
ISBN-10: 1-55870-910-3
7x9, pb, 288 p, #Z0836

...tterway Books titles are available at ...ore or from online suppliers.

WWW.FWBOOKSTORE.COM